SEA
SHEPHERD

by Paul Watson, as told
to Warren Rogers

SEA
SHEPHERD

My Fight for Whales and Seals

Edited by Joseph Newman

Introduction by Cleveland Amory

W · W · NORTON & COMPANY · NEW YORK · LONDON

TITLE PAGE PHOTOGRAPH: Crew member of *Sea Shepherd,* ready to spray a baby seal with harmless red dye. With this technique, over one thousand seals were saved in 1979. *Photograph courtesy of Mary Bloom.*

FIRST EDITION

THE TEXT OF *Sea Shepherd* is composed in photocomposition Baskerville. The display type faces used for the title page, chapters, and other opening pages are Bauer Bodoni Bold, and Craw Modern Bold. Manufacturing is by the Maple-Vail Book Manufacturing Group.

BOOK DESIGN BY MARJORIE J. FLOCK

Library of Congress Cataloging in Publication Data
Watson, Paul.
   Sea Shepherd.
   Includes index.
   1. Watson, Paul.   2. Whale.   3. Seals.   4. Sea
Shepherd (Ship)   5. Conservationists—British
Columbia—Biography.   I. Rogers, Warren.   II. New-
man, Joseph.   III. Title.
QL31.W34A37   1982   333.95′9 [B]   81-14038

ISBN 0-393-01499-1   AACR2

W. W. Norton & Company, Inc. 500 Fifth Avenue, New York, N.Y. 10110
W. W. Norton & Company Ltd. 37 Great Russell Street, London WC1B 3NU

1 2 3 4 5 6 7 8 9 0

FOR MY DAUGHTER, LILLIOLANI

Contents

Illustrations appear following page 130.

Introduction

By Cleveland Amory

WHEN I FORMED The Fund for Animals in 1967, I said at the time that I wanted "to put cleats on the little old ladies in tennis shoes."

I meant no disrespect to humanitarians of an earlier day, to their stature, to their years, to their being of a different sexual persuasion than mine, or even to their choice in footwear. On the contrary, I knew that they, and they alone—often very courageously and in a dark age for animals—kept alight the lamps of decency. They held meetings that were often sparsely attended, formed humane societies, staged protests, and wrote poems.

But I wanted something more. I wanted a tough team able to take on—head on, if need be—the major cruelties to which so many animals are regularly and ruthlessly subjected. That is what I meant by "cleats," and all I meant.

As a matter of fact, many years ago one of these ladies—my dear friend Aida Flemming, of New Brunswick, Canada—formed, for children, North America's first "Kindness Club"; it was this club to which, twenty-three years ago, a young eight-year-old wrote for membership. He was accepted.

His name was Paul Watson. From the beginning, Paul was different. He grew up in an area where many children regularly shot birds, tied tin cans to cats, and put frogs on the street to see how many would be hit by cars. First Paul protested; then, if his protests were not successful, he intervened physically. He was often beaten up, but never beaten down.

As Paul grew older, he thought a lot of other things were also wrong. Not for him the ways of the so-called sportsmen who hunt, trap, and kill. The drummer to whom he marched sought out not the unarmed unequal but rather the contest in which he was himself the unarmed unequal, usually up against hopeless odds. He has paid dearly. He has been beaten and starved, frozen, half-drowned, and imprisoned. But, again, he has never been stopped.

When Paul first wrote to me about his plan to "paint" the seals, and I met him for the first time, I expected the complete "animal nut"—half fanatic, half evangelist. Paul, I soon found, was neither. He was big enough to be a wrestler, but he had the charm of a little boy. He was "Gentle Ben"—with a sense of humor.

Since that time, I have been on network television programs with him; I have also been with him in a lonely jail cell in a foreign country. I have seen him praised to the skies and I have seen him vilified. I have seen him highly publicized and I have seen him totally ignored. He does not change.

When I knew he was determined to ram the pirate whaling ship, *Sierra,* I told him two things. First, he was not to do it in such a way that, afterwards, the two ships would be together. I was afraid the *Sierra* crew would come on board *Sea Shepherd* and kill him. Second, just before the moment of impact, he was to put a mattress in front of him. I thought that not only the bridge but the whole superstructure of *Sea Shepherd* might go over onto the deck.

Paul, of course, always does what I tell him to do. No, make that *sometimes* does what I tell him to do. No, make that *once in a while*. In any case, this time, he did one of the two things—which, for him, is far above average. He did not ram in such a way that the two ships remained together. But he did not, before the ramming, put the mattress in front of him. "I remembered," he told me afterwards, "what you said. But then the other two volunteers, Peter and Jerry, came up on the bridge, and Peter had forgotten his mattress, so I gave him mine."

That is Paul Watson.

Acknowledgments

MY EFFORTS TO PROTECT WILDLIFE, especially marine mammals, have been successful because of the support and encouragement of many people. Without Cleveland Amory and The Fund for Animals, I would never have been able to sail the *Sea Shepherd* to a glorious victory over pirate whaling. Cleveland is a great humanitarian, and I feel honored that he has written the introduction to this book.

Thanks are also due to all the people of The Fund for Animals. In particular, I would like to thank Marian Probst, Lewis Regenstein, Edward Walsh, Glenn Chase, Margaret Morey, Marlene Lakin, Donna Gregory, and Cynthia Branigan.

A captain is only as good as his crew, and some of my crewmembers contributed more in the way of courage and dedication than I can express. Without my Australian chief engineer, Peter Woof, there would have been no victory over that infamous pirate whaler, the *Sierra*. When others retreated in the face of danger, Jerry Doran, my third engineer, stood beside Peter and me. These two were the very best.

Others who sailed and served with distinction were Captain David Sellers from Scotland and Captain Leslie Fewster from Yorkshire; crewmembers Al Johnson,

David McColl, David MacKenney, Mark Sterk, Keith Krueger, Matt Herron, Paul Pezwick, Tina Harrison, and Tony Watson. Reporters Sid Moody, Larry Manning, and Sunny Lewis, in addition to fulfilling their journalistic obligations, were not above helping out in an emergency.

Many people helped to finance our campaigns: Dr. William Jordan of the Royal Society for the Prevention of Cruelty to Animals; Clare Albert, Christopher Roof and the many supporting and charter members of the Sea Shepherd Society in North America, Europe, and Australia. I am grateful to many British groups—The League Against Cruel Sports, The Portsmouth Save the Whales Action Group, The Black Country Anti-Whaling Group, and the Hunt Saboteurs. In Canada, we have been helped by Aida Flemming and her Kindness Club, by the Canadians for the Abolition of the Seal Hunt and by the Action Volunteers Association.

A special thank-you to my wife, Starlet, for enduring sea sickness, storms, and a thousand other problems we encountered together during our struggle to protect and conserve life.

Finally, I would like to acknowledge the whales, dolphins, seals, elephants, and all the other creatures on this Earth whom I have been honored to serve. Their beauty, intelligence, strength, and spirit have inspired me. These beings have spoken to me, touched me, and I have been rewarded by friendship with many members of different species.

If the whales survive and flourish, if the seals continue to live and give birth, and if I can contribute in ensuring their future prosperity, I will be forever happy.

PAUL WATSON

1

To Save the Whales

I WAS THE LEAD *kamikaze.* We had found what we had
come for, some sixty miles off San Francisco in the
Pacific Ocean. And now we rocketed toward the Soviet
whaling pirates in our outboard-powered, inflatable
rubber Zodiacs, hearts pounding and adrenalin pump-
ing. After two months at sea, enduring hardships none
of us had expected, we had won our gamble against the
odds. We had tracked down the killer fleet—six small
ships, one huge one—and it loomed before us, closer
each second, as we popped and skimmed across the
choppy waves at forty miles per hour.

Robert Hunter, journalist and ecologist, leader of
our expedition to save the whales, stood just in front of
me. Legs apart and knees flexed, feet planted firmly on
the wood deckplate of our little rubber horseshoe, he
clung to the bowline like a water skier. He was a wild,
strange sight in his black wetsuit, eyes glinting and long
hair flying from under a rainbow-colored Peruvian hat.
He seemed threatening even in the bright sunlight—a
dark figure carved on the prow of a marauding Viking
ship. I crouched close behind him, leaning forward on
my right elbow, left hand thrust back to the controls of
the roaring outboard, craning to see what lay ahead.

Bob Hunter swiveled around. He looked me over

and gave out a laugh that wound up a shout. Later, he
would tell me he thought we both looked weird, I no
less than he in my blue wetsuit and with my own mop of
unruly hair restrained by a white *banzai* scarf, its loose
ends flapping madly in our slipstream. I had adopted
the head scarf from Japanese warrior culture because
sooner or later we would be throwing our tiny *kamikaze*
fleet at the illegal whalers of Japan—the only other outlaw country in this field besides the Soviet Union—and
I wanted the Japanese to know how serious we were
about stopping the killing.

I did not care how weird or strange we looked now.
And neither, I knew, did Bob Hunter. What mattered
to us, and mattered desperately, was that our voyage for
peace and the ecology by our Greenpeace Foundation,
was bound to win. As we had promised our members
and other supporters (plus all who cared enough to note
our statements and posters distributed throughout the
United States and Canada), we were on our way to put
our bodies between the Soviet harpoonists and the
sperm whales they were systematically and illegally
slaughtering. And we would have proof, not only
through our eyewitness accounts of what we saw and
heard, but especially through the incontrovertible evidence for all the world of our still photographs and
movie film. That was our mission, and we were fulfilling
it.

As if on signal, Bob reached back and I reached forward. Our eyes met and held and our hands clasped.
We said almost the same thing at the same time.

"We're here! It's happening! We're doing it!"

"We're doing it, Paul! We're doing it!"

Behind us came two other Zodiacs in the little *kamikaze* fleet under my command. It had been Bob

Hunter's idea to get between the harpoons and whales. When he asked me for technical suggestions on how to do it, I remembered these super-fast rubber inflatables, only fourteen feet long and about five feet wide. They skittered over water like a flat stone flung by a schoolboy across a mill pond. I had ridden other such collapsible speedboats, but nothing among them could compare to these amazing craft developed by Jacques Cousteau and his people in their oceanographic research. They were unsinkable marvels of design and a thrill to operate— and I knew, too, a major weapon in our propaganda battle with the Soviet and Japanese outlaw fleets. Their speed and size and maneuverability allowed us to take ourselves and our cameras into pointblank range between the harpoonist and the whale, to gather denial-proof evidence. Credibility was our big gun, and the Zodiacs helped provide it.

I looked back at the other two Zodiacs of my tiny flotilla of the "divine wind" (the literal meaning of *kamikaze*). Closer to me was the boat piloted by Dr. Patrick Moore, with Fred Easton manning the moving-picture cameras, and, straggling behind, lucky to have made it at all, came the other boat with George Korotva in command and Rex Weyler braced in the bow, several still cameras dangling from his neck plus another in his hand and ready for snapping. Moore, with a Ph.D. in environmental studies, was our shipboard ecologist when not running a Zodiac; Korotva, the only crew member besides myself and Captain John Cormack with prior experience at sea, was expected to conduct whatever conversation we might have with the Soviet whalers. A Czechoslovakian, he had learned Russian in the Siberian work camp he had been shipped to after his arrest for participating in the 1965 student uprisings in

Prague. He had escaped to Finland eighteen months later, knocked about Europe for a while, and made his way eventually to Canada. We all hoped his Russian was better than his English, which was terrible. He had a habit of putting "the" in front of everything, and so we naturally called him "The George." But he was no mean mariner. At thirty-three, he had already skippered bigger craft than our eighty-seven-foot halibut seine-fisher, the *Phyllis Cormack.*

So much had happened to us since we had left port exactly sixty days earlier—on Sunday, April 27, 1975—that it was surprising to find our enthusiasm for our mission undiminished. The six of us, like the seven others on board the *Phyllis Cormack*, were physically bedraggled by the rigors of our search up and down and around some three thousand square miles of the Pacific Ocean, straining our eyes for a glimpse of our quarry and bending our ears to the scratch and squawk of the boat's old radio for some hint of a Russian accent that would tip us off. But, thanks to our youth (most of us were in our twenties and thirties) and our dedication to the cause of saving whales, our spirits seemed as high as when we had left Jericho Beach in the port of Vancouver in Canada's British Columbia—with more than twenty thousand well-wishers gathered there to cheer us on.

We were reasonably confident we could accomplish the first step in our mission, simply going out on the Pacific Ocean and finding the Soviet whalers. Through a variety of fund-raising activities, ranging from jiggling tincans outside liquor stores to staging huge benefit concerts, we had managed to put together the finances for the voyage—money to rent the *Phyllis Cormack* again (she had been the vessel on the first Greenpeace foray in 1971, an ill-starred and ultimately aborted effort to halt United States nuclear testing in the National Wildlife Refuge at Amchitka Island in the Aleutian chain by sailing into the test area) and to assemble the vast array of necessities—Zodiacs, life jackets, radios, wetsuits, diving tanks, hydrophones, and all the rest, including fuel and food. We had done well in fund-raising, so much so that the *Phyllis Cormack*, which had looked more than a bit scruffy the first time out, was a thing of beauty when we gathered at Jericho Beach for the speechmaking, partying, and general merrymaking associated with a grand and glorious sendoff. We had painted her a pristine white, with glossy green and black accents, and, instead of the grimy, workaday green sail of the first trip, this time she boasted a snowy, spanking-new canvas triangle crisply imprinted with the great sea wolf symbol of the Kwakiutl Indians of Vancouver Island.

But more than our sense of physical preparedness enlivened our hopes for success. We had acquired some intelligence about where the Soviet whaling fleet was likely to be in that forbiddingly trackless expanse of ocean into which we were sailing. One of our number, Dr. Paul Spong, who had been traveling to help raise money, managed to gain access to the records of the Bureau of International Whaling Statistics in Sandefjord, Norway. There, in data going back to 1938, when orderly statistics-keeping first began for whaling, Spong found all we needed to know about recent activities of the Soviet and Japanese whalers. He copied out thirteen pages that showed longitudes and latitude, dates, and slaughter figures for the Soviet factory ships *Dalniy Vostok* and *Vladivostok* and the Japanese ships *Nissim Maru 3*, *Tonan Maru 2*, and *Kukuyo Maru 3* from August 1973 to October 1974. Thus armed with a profile of the past two years, we knew pretty much where the killing grounds were. But it would still be a needle-in-the-haystack proposition to plunge into the area and find the killers.

The axe-bit bow of the *Phyllis Cormack* had kicked out a graceful wash as we moved through moderately heavy seas—vestiges of a sudden storm that had lashed the coast and obscured the full moon of the night before we had launched from Jericho Bay on that last Sunday in April. Captain John Cormack was in fine fettle. Much older than the rest of us, he was, at sixty-three, less an environmental activist than a dedicated disciple of the work ethic who would rather be on charter with us than idled back in Vancouver by a summer of poor fishing. He seemed to have cast himself in the surly-old-sea-dog role, grumbling at every deviation from his standards of deportment, and he maintained a strict and uncompromised distance between his station as skipper and ours as the chartering crew. Captain Cormack had a deep and abiding affection for the *Phyllis Cormack,* which he had named after his wife, and he was inordinately proud of her new look—the result of nearly a quarter of a million dollars in repairs, including a brand-new Caterpillar diesel engine. The skipper made a point of disassociating himself from our goals. Yet, I had the feeling he thoroughly enjoyed the part he contributed to the protest—as a hired functionary who committed his skills but not necessarily his heart to the cause—and secretly approved of what we were trying to do, if not of how.

"Just point where you want to go," he would grunt, his stocky frame exuding confidence as he took the wheel, "and I'll get you there."

We were in no hurry, that first day out of Vancouver, to head south for where we knew the Soviet and Japanese whalers would be operating. The information provided by Dr. Spong indicated it would be toward the end of June—nearly eight weeks away—before the killer ships would be within the range of the *Phyllis Cormack*. We had received this information too late to postpone the big sendoff planned for us on April 27—a ceremony also designed to raise further contributions— and so we went ahead as scheduled. We would fill in the intervening days by practicing with our little Zodiac *kamikazes*, publicizing our search as much as possible through news releases out of Vancouver via our boat's radio, and attempting some highly unscientific experiments in communicating with any whales, porpoises, dolphins, or other cetaceans we might encounter.

Al Hewitt, tall, lean, and taciturn, with expressive, busy eyebrows, was our chief communicator. He had assembled a wide range of electronic gear, much of it stored in a four-man aluminum trailer mounted on the poop deck. It was essentially a sound studio, crammed with speakers, oscilloscopes, generators, tape decks, microphones, headphones, transistors, capacitors, and walkie-talkies. A quadraphonic underwater sound system was set between the trailer and a half-dozen cylindrical hydrophones about four feet long. Captain Cormack scoffed at any hopes of having "a chit-chat with whales," but we told him we did not see any harm in trying. Later, he relented somewhat, partly because of his great respect for the thirty-seven-year-old Hewitt's electronic and engineering capabilities and partly because we explained that considerable serious experimentation was underway in "interspecies communication."

Perhaps the most outrageous story I know on this

subject is the old yarn that Norwegian sailors tell. It seems a bishop of Nidaros held a seaside service on what he thought was a rock, but what was actually the back of a sleeping kraken (a mythological cave-dwelling monster probably based on the giant squid, which can measure sixty feet and weigh a couple of thousand pounds). The kraken awoke while the old man was speaking but found the sermon so eloquent that he politely kept still until the bishop had stopped talking, packed up his altar and left.

We knew something about *ketophonation,* the name given to the phenomenon of vibrations produced by whales and that some call "singing." This song of the whales has been recorded and studied by marine biologists and other scientists for years. In World War II, when the Allies were desperate for information on echo-locating, which is essentially sonar, studies were carried out to learn new and better methods of coping with submarine warfare. Since then, underwater sounds made by whales, porpoises, dolphins squid, fishes, crabs, shrimps, and a host of other creatures have been the subject of countless scientific reports. That cetaceans use a kind of sonar in navigating the world's great bodies of water is no longer in question. With hearing attuned to frequencies as high as 200 kilohertz, compared to the human limit of 20, they are clearly well-equipped for sonar, and scientists have established that cetaceans not only distinguish between the sizes of small-food fish but also determine whether a net is of coarse or fine mesh.

As for the intelligence of cetaceans, no scientific study has yet proved to what extent they are able to think—as humans think. However, considerable evidence exists that porpoises exhibit emotional and motivational responses higher than those of dogs and close to those of chimpanzees. Weight ratios are interesting, if inconclusive: an adult human's brain, the center of reason, weighs about three pounds, roughly fifty times the weight of the spinal cord, which controls reflexive behavior; in apes, the brain-to-cord ratio is eight to one, but, surprisingly, porpoises show a close-to-human ratio of thirty-six to one. It is known, too, that dolphins engage in "polite" conversation—that is, they make noises in patterns that resemble vocal exchanges during which one party "talks" only during the silence of the other. Further, in captivity, dolphins adapt the sounds they make. Like strangers in a new land, they modify their noises until, no less than parrots, they seem to be speaking the language of their human captors. What kind of brain is there, to be met and explored by some mutually comprehensible means of communication?

We chopped through the heavy swells of the Strait of Juan de Fuca coming out of Puget Sound and watched Cape Flattery fall behind us as we sailed north for Tofino on Vancouver Island. There, we picked up our cameramen before continuing north to Winter Harbour on Quatsino Sound at the northern tip of the island. The seas were so rough it took us five days for a journey we should have made in two or three. It was at Winter Harbour, too, that the *Phyllis Cormack* rendezvoused with the *Vega,* another veteran of Greenpeace operations, which would be joining us for a while in the initial stages of our search for the Soviet whalers.

During my years as an activist, I have been emotionally and spiritually torn between the opposing philosophies of violence and nonviolence. Morally, I know, violence is wrong and nonviolence is right. But what about results? What obtains the most results with the least amount of delay and obfuscation?

The path chosen by the North American Indian is the most comprehensive example of nonviolence I can think of. After the massacre at Wounded Knee in the 1890s, which until recently we had all been taught was a justified action and a great victory for the United States Army, until the resistance at Wounded Knee in 1973 (in which I personally participated) the Indian had passively accepted his lot. When he sought justice—or changes in the system so that it might breed justice—he did so through peaceful means. Those rare but exceedingly publicized occasions when he turned reluctantly to violence were far, far less frequent than his peaceful efforts. His reward has been generations of broken vows solemnly given, and rejection, abuse, racism, and cultural genocide. Only in our time, with the rise of the North American Indian movement, has the world at least begun to recognize the reality of his existence and the validity of his rights.

Few changes on this planet have taken place solely because of nonviolent action. To remain nonviolent totally is to allow the perpetuation of violence against people, animals, and the environment. The Catch-22 of it—the damned-if-you-do-damned-if-you-don't dilemma—is that, if we eschew violence for ourselves, we often thereby tacitly allow violence for others, who are then free to settle issues violently until they are resisted, necessarily with violence. Yet, violence is wrong, regardless of its source or purpose.

And so the search for compromise goes on. I have progressed in my thinking since 1975 to this: sometimes, to dramatize a point so that effective steps may follow, it is necessary to perform a violent act. But such violence must never be directed against a living thing. Against property, yes. But never against a life.

However, I must confess that, in May 1975, I was not thinking such philosophical thoughts as we continued to make ready for our run at the Soviet whalers. What I was thinking of, precisely, was my stomach. Rarely have I had such a series of sharp, stabbing pains, deep down on the right side of my abdomen. Dr. Myron McDonald, a member of our crew, made a quick diagnosis of appendicitis, and I was taken by helicopter out of Winter Harbour to Campbell River on the east coast of Vancouver Island, where the diagnosis was confirmed and an operation performed to rid me of the inflamed appendix.

But I was afraid of losing my place aboard the *Phyllis Cormack*. Two days after the operation, I checked out of the hospital. I drove over to Vancouver and then out to Tofino on the Pacific coast of the island because I knew that was where the boat was scheduled to begin experiments that would test the possibilities of communicating with whales. I had studied interspecies communication in college and, while I knew that confrontation with the Soviet whalers was our overriding mission, I looked forward to any attempts to reach out to the whales themselves. Sure enough, at Tofino I learned the *Phyllis Cormack* had gone out to consort with a pod of gray whales, and I could see her about a mile offshore at Long Beach.

I put on my wetsuit and went into the water. Immediately, I was caught in an undertow. It pulled my legs from under me like some giant, invisible hand, and I kept still, trying to maintain my balance, as it drew me swiftly away from shore. I had had the experience before, and I was not alarmed. I knew I could get out of

it, as I had before. But this time was different. At even
the mildest exertion I would feel an excruciating stab in
my lower abdomen, and I had visions of my two-day-old
scar bursting open to spill out my life in the Pacific
Ocean. At one point I wondered if I might do better *au
naturel* and I started to peel off my wetsuit—it was keeping me buoyant, which made it difficult for me to get
my bearings and robbed me of full power to swim—but
the water was too cold. My hand, without a glove, went
numb and useless in the frigid water and started turning blue. I replaced the glove and floundered on. And
then I figured out a way to get myself out of the fix I
was in. It took half an hour but it worked: I waited for
a wave, and, when it came, I dove to the bottom,
plunged my diving knife into the sand, and then hung
on against the outward sucking of the water. When I
felt that subside, I rose to the surface, gulped air, and
dove to the bottom again with the help of the next
onrushing wave. Over and over, in rhythm with the
waves, I repeated the process, "walking" my way to
shore, until I staggered out, holding my tortured side
and happy to be alive.

I had missed out on what indeed had been a day of
excitement for the crew of the *Phyllis Cormack.* As the
boat rounded the peninsula into the broad bay of Long
Beach on the West Coast of Vancouver Island, my
colleagues saw the tell-tale feather of white vapor spurt-
ing off the surface, and then another and another. All
told, there were eight gray whales (*Eschrichtius robustus*)
feeding hungrily in the shallows on a stop in their
migration up and down the Pacific Coast: from Vancouver Island, where the waters began to get too cold for
their taste, to the mellower temperatures of Baja California and Mexico. By international agreement since

1938, the grays presumably have been protected. But their numbers now are a little over ten thousand, and the Asiatic gray, which used to breed off the coast of Korea, is virtually extinct.

My colleagues had quickly launched the four Zodiacs among the grays, loading up with cameras, including special equipment for underwater photography, and various musical instruments for testing communication. A flute, a saxophone, and even a synthesizer (set up and operated by Will Jackson from Al Hewitt's electronics-jammed aluminum trailer aboard the *Phyllis Cormack*) aimed a kaleidoscope of sounds at the grays. Some of them occasionally seemed to be listening, although it was impossible to say so with certainty. The whales, gentle beasts that they are, allowed the Zodiacs to come among them, even to make some contact. The smell was a bit of a surprise. As Bob Hunter reported: "Afterward, everyone agreed that the gray whales had the equivalent of halitosis." One Zodiac—bearing Gary Zimmerman (who was to leave for another assignment before we sailed out to meet the Soviets), photographer Rex Weyler, and pig-tailed Carlie Trueman (scuba and small-craft expert, and our only female)—managed to maneuver up to a gray estimated to be about fifty feet long. Suddenly, the three felt their rubber boat coming up out of the water. The whale had used its tail to raise them a foot above the surface before letting them gently back down. They took it as a warning and moved away.

By the middle of June, after forays into the open Pacific and north to the Queen Charlotte Islands, we were ready to go after the Soviet whalers in earnest. It was nearly the end of June—the time Paul Spong had calculated would offer the best chance of finding them.

To improve our chances by increasing our range, we had arranged for Rod Marining and our other people in Vancouver to meet us at Winter Harbour and outfit us with eight 250-gallon fuel tanks. We expected them to add a thousand miles to our range.

When we set sail from Winter Harbour on June 18, we felt ready. We had mastered the Zodiacs and were now skilled at racing just ahead of the *Phyllis Cormack*, simulating what we would do under the bow of the Soviet whaler when we interposed ourselves between the harpoon gun and the whale that was its prey. Captain Cormack, who proved to be an aggressive competitor, played the role of the whaler well, narrowly avoiding running us down on occasion. We also had more adventures with whales, coming upon three finbacks (*Balaenoptera physalus*) one day, and, another time, observing and filming the copulation of a pair of "killer" whales, the much-maligned black-and-white orca (*Grampus orca*). These are no more killers than any other animal that must hunt to live, and they are not whales at all but large dolphins. As Dr. Victor B. Scheffer, the celebrated American authority on marine mammals, has pointed out, "killer" is the name that men have given these creatures, not a name they gave themselves. The greatest killer of all is *Homo sapiens.*

What we did not know, as we sailed expectantly out to sea, was that, while Paul Spong had been able to tell us where the Soviet whalers would *generally* be, the Russians were aware at all times *exactly* where we were. Chalk it up to our *naïveté* or the perfidy of governments or both, but that was the situation. During our operating around the Queen Charlottes, we had put in at Massett on the chain's northernmost shores, site of a Canadian Air Force base. There, we had a dialogue with a Canadian Air Force officer that went something like this:

"I hear you're after the Russian whalers. Maybe we can help you."

"Oh? What can you do?"

"We can give you the positions."

"That's fine! That's great!"

"Sure. All you have to do is give us your position every day."

And so we obliged. Not only was that a one-way street but we found out later the Canadian Air Force was turning over the information to the Soviet embassy in Ottawa. That made it possible for the Soviets to know where we were at all times, and we never heard a whisper from the Canadian Air Force about where the whalers were. Obviously, the Canadian government did not want a confrontation between us and the Soviets on the high seas. A generous interpretation would be that Ottawa wanted to protect us from harm and to avoid whatever embarrassment might accrue for the two governments involved. But we did not enjoy being "had" by the Canadian Air Force. Somebody once said a diplomat is an honest man sent abroad to lie for his country. To that we might add that, somewhere in its air force, Canada has, if you will pardon the pun, one whale of a diplomat.

As we made our way south, at the *Phyllis Cormack*'s ladylike five to eight knots, it seemed to me that Bob Hunter, as project leader, had assembled a worthy crew—resourceful and dedicated. Crusty old John Cormack, the owner of the boat and its skipper, was a steadying influence. George Korotva and I had considerable sea service, and, while I had picked up a little Russian in a college course, George was fairly fluent. Also, Patrick

Moore was a trained ecologist, Al Hewitt was our electronics-communications wizard, Rex Weyler our still photographer, Fred Easton our movie cameraman, Carlie Trueman our small-boat expert, Walrus Oakenbough (originally David Garrick before he chose his new name in a moment of determined whimsy only to drop it later) our cook and sharpest-eyed lookout, and Melville Gregory, Will Jackson, and Ron Precious in a variety of backup roles.

To tell the truth, though, none of us was feeling up to par. After nearly two months, despite our failure to locate the Soviets, our spirits were high, but we were physically down. The extra diesel fuel we had stored aboard had leaked out in the hold. We found tinned food floating in it, labels soaked off, and cardboard boxes of fresh fruit collapsed in a soggy mess of oil and bilge water. We took everything topside and washed it as best we could. But after that, everything we ate tasted of diesel oil, everything we touched had diesel oil on it, everything smelled of diesel oil, and every time we burped, which was often because of our ever-present nausea, we burped up diesel fumes. If there is such a thing as getting used to misery, and I suppose there is, we were learning how.

We found some whales, nine finbacks, and we launched Zodiacs to get a closer look. With our cameras going, Korotva maneuvered our Zodiac close to a large mother whale whose baby was swimming serenely at her side. My intention was to leap from the boat and swim along with the mother whale as the cameras recorded it all. But she gave a sudden, mighty flap of her flukes on the ocean surface, and I knew it was time to clear out. Korotva cut the engine and the whales moved on past us.

Coincidental with that meeting we learned on our boat's radio that a moratorium on the killing of finbacks had been proposed at the 1975 International Whaling Commission meeting, which had convened in London on June 22. We were delighted with the coincidence and agreed it would be wonderful if, somehow, our confrontation with the Soviets would have some impact on the IWC deliberations. Even so, we were too realistic to hope for much.

The IWC began functioning in 1948 for the purpose of rebuilding the whaling industry, which had been severely disrupted during World War II. It is dominated by the whaling industry, not by governments, and, although man has hunted whales as long as he has known them, nothing can match the carnage since the IWC has been in existence. Huge fleets abetted by sonar, helicopters, factory ships, explosive harpoons, and all such modern-day technologies have decimated the populations of the eight species of great whales until they are all threatened with extinction. The whale killers—mainly Japan and the Soviet Union—blithely ignore the toothless sanctions adopted at each annual IWC meeting.

And the ultimate irony is that, while the slaughter goes on at the rate of one whale killed every twenty minutes, anything that these warm-blooded, air-breathing, milk-giving creatures provide to mankind can be duplicated from other sources. And that includes cosmetics, pet food, fuel oil, steaks that sell for twenty dollars per pound in Tokyo, and the fine oil that the Soviets use to lubricate their intercontinental ballistic missiles.

Herman Melville may have said it all in *Moby Dick* when he wrote: "The moot point is, whether Leviathan can long endure so wide a chase, and so remorseless a havoc; whether he must not at last be exterminated from the waters, and the last whale, like the last man, smoke his last pipe, and then himself evaporate in the final puff."

We had been hearing Russian voices on our boat radio almost since turning south from Tofino. But we could never tell whether they were from ordinary drag-fishers working just outside the twelve-mile territorial limit off the California coast, or from our quarry, the whalers. On June 25, we came in among a massive fleet—dozens of hulking, rusting ships that were Soviet and Polish draggers. Closer to shore, within the continental limit, were smaller, wooden boats—the American fishermen—and we went over to one of these: a forty-foot trawler named *Tilko*. We were welcomed aboard and allowed to use the radio, ours being down for repairs again, and we made a call to Eureka, California, patched through to Greenpeace Foundation headquarters in Vancouver. It was then we learned the bad news that Canada had joined with Japan and the Soviet Union to vote to increase whale quotas at the IWC session in London.

Friday, June 27, 1975, dawned in a calming peace. On watch at the wheel, enjoying the pleasant if diesel-tainted smell of buckweat pancakes drifting from the galley to the wheelhouse, I took note idly as the orange fire of the sun came up out of the blue-gray of the Pacific. A short burst of Russian broke through the sputter and buzz of our poor little radio, which had been a bargain, like all the rest of our second-hand or cut-rate equipment for which we had shopped on our limited budget. George Korotva, coffee mug in hand, ran to the radio room and talked to Al Hewitt; he fiddled with the dials of his radio direction finder—definitely his, for he had been nursing it along for two months. He was a magician with soldering iron and clothes-hanger wire. Al got a precise fix, and I swung the wheel a few degrees to port as we continued northwestward—emboldened because, for some time, Korotva had been insisting he could make out the word, "*Vostok*," in radio chatter, and that, we all knew, could be the factory ship of the Soviet whaling fleet.

With my watch over, I surrendered the wheel to Mel Gregory and stumbled below for pancakes and a good sleep. The RDF needle was strong for a while, telling us that, somewhere out there, as it had been for days, was a radio spouting Russian. Was it the factory ship called *Vostok*? And how far was it? Ten miles? A hundred?

And then I heard Mel Gregory's shout from the wheelhouse. It jerked my head off the pillow and sent all of us scurrying about to our stations.

"Whalers! Wha-a-lers! Holy Christ, they're whalers!"

We had found her, the factory ship *Dalniy Vostok*. At 750 feet long and about ten stories high, she looked like some terribly abused and abandoned old spaceship out of the movie *Star Wars*. And we could make out the killer ships, too—much smaller but no less battered and bruised, with their unmistakably characteristic catwalk from bridge to bow, where the cannon with its explosive harpoons sat menacingly on the forepeak. As we got into wetsuits and readied our Zodiacs, gusts of wind from the direction of the fleet brought traces of a musky odor. Anyone who has ever gone past a slaughterhouse would know it. But the full horror was yet to come.

Still on the horizon, the fleet busied itself, its 150-foot-long killer boats darting around their massive mother, giving off bursts of smoke as they changed speed and direction. They were collecting their dead and delivering them to the factory. The kills were marked with red triangular flags, with a radio beacon attached to guide the killer boats back to them.

Suddenly, we were aware of a blue-gray mass off our starboard bow. It was a whale carcass, duly marked, bobbing on the shallow waves. No Leviathan, this, but a very young sperm whale, below the size allowed by IWC agreement. My first thought, as I went into my Zodiac to get closer, was that we had caught the Soviets red-handed in violation of the IWC limitation.

"My God!" Carlie Trueman cried. "It's only a baby!"

From my boat, I went into the water and paddled up to the still form. Its skin was still warm, and oily to the touch. Blood seemed to be flowing from a gaping wound on its side and it felt warm on my hand. I stroked the flipper. Below the waves, the great jaw flapped rhythmically with the motion of the sea, opening and closing softly like a great gate. The whale child, I calculated (and the photographs later confirmed), measured twenty-three feet—seven feet below IWC regulation limit. I felt lost and lonely upon the ocean with that dead whale child. I reached up and slowly closed the lid over its vacantly staring eye.

Back aboard the *Phyllis Cormack,* we pushed on until we came in among the Soviets. It was a scene out of Dante's *Inferno.* Gore flowed across the deck of the *Dalniy Vostok* as the whales, once magnificent creatures of the deep, were hauled tail-first by great claws and cables up the slipways to the flensing deck. From the scuppers ran rivers of red, cascading into the blue seas and staining them to purple. Reddish trails came across the water in the *Dalniy Vostok*'s wake and tainted the shiny white of the *Phyllis Cormack*'s hull. And all about us sharks darted nervously, tasting the water and hoping, perhaps, for more solid fare.

As I watched the killer ships nuzzle up to the rear of the *Dalniy Vostok* and wait until their catches were hoisted into the great, square maw of its stern, I had a disgusting thought: It is like a feeding! What manner of beast is it that feeds through its anus?

Surprisingly, the crew of the factory ship, high above the barbarism of the flensing deck, were at the rails on the uppermost level. They had been playing volleyball and were sunning themselves—even a woman, incongruously wearing a bikini swimsuit. Apparently much surprised to see our little boat so far out to sea, they waved cheerfully. Cameras came out and they snapped pictures of us as fast as we took pictures of them.

Korotva, now called upon to perform his role as interpreter, held tightly to the railing of our boat and yelled up to the Soviet crewmen. In effect, he was calling upon them to join with the Greenpeace Foundation and the fifty-three nations that voted for a ten-year moratorium on commercial whaling at a United Nations conference on the human environment at Stockholm in June, 1972. He urged the crewmen to stop killing whales.

When he had finished, one of the Soviets yelled something, and we asked George to translate.

"He says go get fokked."

We could no longer stand the stench. Some of our crew had been to the rail as soon as we drew near the *Dalniy Vostok*. I could feel my stomach heaving and cold sweat on my brow. After three hours of following and filming, we broke away. We had seen well over three dozen great sperms being converted into the raw material of shoe polish and lipstick and other things the Soviet government considers more vital to mankind than the continuation of whales on this earth.

We had seen, photographed, and filmed the Soviet factory ship in action. Now, we had one more thing to do, which was the main purpose of our journey to the open reaches of the Pacific. We had to put ourselves between the whale and the harpoon and, if that would not save a whale, at least we would have a filmed record for our indictment of these pirates.

Breaking off with the *Dalniy Vostok* amid jeers and rude gesticulations from her crew, we set out behind the last of the killer ships. We could not keep pace. Our top speed of eight knots was no match for its twenty knots. Soon, it was over the horizon. But we plowed on. Another killer ship caught up with us and passed on, and another and another. At least we knew we were generally headed in the right direction. A fourth caught up, and the gunner sitting in the bow playfully aimed his harpoon-launcher at us, and then it, too, was out of sight.

And then, from the top of our mast, where he had been perched for three hours, scanning the seas all about, Walrus Oakenbough let out a scream:

"Whales!"

Bob Hunter and I, like the others chafing in our wet-suits, were into our Zodiacs and roaring away in what seemed like seconds. So were Pat Moore and Fred Easton with their movie equipment; Fred was worried about running out of film after all of his shooting earlier. But George Korotva and Rex Weyler, armed to the teeth with cameras, were in trouble. Their outboard motor would not start. Will Jackson jumped into the hold and, with one great heave, lifted the two hundred-

pound spare motor to the deck. Captain Cormack
caught it and thumped it down and then over the side
to Korotva, who caught it, set it in place, got it going,
and roared off in pursuit of the other two boats. It was
a great testimonial to the power of adrenalin.

At full throttle, Bob and I sped under the bow of a
killer ship. The Soviet crew members looked at us curi-
ously, wondering, it seemed, what in the world we were
up to. With a pod of whales before us, the harpoon
behind us, we knew what we were doing. I was having
one of the most magnificent visual experiences of my
life. A dozen feet before our craft swam ten ocean behe-
moths, racing and spouting, coursing easily through the
choppy seas. Behind us a man stood behind a gun bearing a 250-pound explosive harpoon.

A thrill of excitement engulfed my entire body. Bob
and I were laughing at the harpoon. Yet, we were
laughing too soon. Our outboard sputtered, coughed
and died.

Relentlessly, the rusty, scaly bow of the killer ship
came at us. Soviet seamen at the rail laughed and jeered
and waved their fists. It seemed we would surely be run
down. But the Zodiac bobbed like a cork on the ship's
bow wave and, with only feet to spare, we were thrust
aside. The captain on the bridge, looking down at us,
curled his lips into a contemptuous grin and drew a
forefinger across his throat. Up forward, the harpooner
watched us float by and then turned back to his task.

The other two Zodiacs came rushing up, and Bob
jumped out of mine and into Korotva's. Easton left
Korotva and joined me in my drifting craft. I swore at
the motor and gave it a vicious rap with my fist. To my
utter surprise, it sputtered into action. George and Bob
had already gone off to join Moore and Weyler between

the harpoon and the whales, and, in quick order, we were with them, too—all three Zodiacs racing together, with George and Bob in the lead and us flanking them.

Suddenly, the lead Zodiac fell into a trough while the whales and whaler rode high on swells. It was a perfect shot, over the Zodiac and into a whale. A crisp explosion rang out, reverberating across the seas. The harpoon, over four feet long, flew over the heads of Bob and George. It buried itself with a sickening *thwap!* in a female sperm. The line attached to it splashed into the water a few feet away from the lead Zodiac. Deep within the whale, the harpoon exploded, driving shrapnel into her vital organs, shredding muscle, shattering bone. We heard her scream. And we saw her mate go at once to her side, roaring as he spun toward her.

Through the ages, sperm whales have been known to attack boats. It is said they are the only whales that do. Perhaps it is a territorial instinct, or the sperm's great size that makes him fear nothing, no matter how big. Now, with an attack on his mate, the male had cause to add to instinct.

With a complete turn, the bull went past our small boats and threw himself with great force against the steel bow of the killer ship. Harpooned when he attacked, he roared again and slid back into the water, bleeding heavily from his great head.

He hesitated there, appearing to gather himself for another lunge. But the harpoon had spent him. His head seemed to loll weakly as he raised himself up, up, higher and higher, up out of the water. His breath came in spouts of pinkish mist, and blood flowed profusely from his mouth, which flapped as if he were gasping for life.

He rose slowly out of the water, a quarter of his bulk

towering above us. His eye fell upon Fred and me, two tiny men in a little rubber raft, and he looked at us. It was a gaze, a gentle, knowing, forgiving gaze. Slowly, slowly, as if he did not want to disturb the water unduly, as if taking care that his great tail did not scrape us from our little perch, he settled into the quietly lapping waves. I had one more glimpse of that gazing eye, and then he was gone from our world.

What had I seen? Was it understanding? We wept, there in that boat on that ocean, we wept—for the whales and for ourselves.

I am not a mystical man, although there are many things that have happened to me that I cannot explain, things that do not fit easily into the pattern of logical and practical reasoning that I inherited from my French and Scottish-English and Scandinavian forebears. I no longer try to understand what happened between that dying Sperm bull and me. I know only that I felt a commitment. This whale, like hundreds of thousands of others in my lifetime, had died at the hands of men. But his dying was different. This death of a whale I had attended, and I owed something.

2

Call of the Sea

ALL OF US ABOARD THE *Phyllis Cormack* were fired up as we left the Soviet whaling fleet's killing grounds and sailed into San Francisco with our own catch—scores of still photographs and yard upon yard of sound movie film. Even our cynical sea dog, Captain John Cormack, seemed enthusiastic. After all the weeks of frustration and hardship, it was a joy to be lionized by the American press upon arrival. We, who were used to a supplicant's role with the Canadian press, radio, and television, now had to adjust to a sudden rush of American reporters who demanded details of our exploit. The derring-do of putting ourselves between the whales and the harpoon, plus fully documenting the Soviets' piratical flaunting of regulations of the International Whaling Commission, had captured the imagination of the American news media.

We relished our moment of success and celebrity. We felt we had achieved the highest of high ground in publicizing the event when we found ourselves with several minutes on Walter Cronkite's "Evening News" over Columbia Broadcasting System's national network. Our footage, including the actual sight and sound of the firing of the harpoon over the Zodiacs and into the whale, especially the *cra-a-ack!* of the gun at the launch, was shown by Cronkite and picked up by others and used around the world. This footage has been shown many times over the years and remains to this day one of the strongest indictments of Soviet disregard for world opinion in pursuit of the destruction of the whale. In addition to the excellent TV coverage, stories illustrated with our photographs appeared in hundreds of newspapers and magazines. A few years later, in 1978, our film of the voyage, *To Save a Whale,* won a Canadian documentary award in its category.

As a result of our experience, it became standard procedure for activists in Zodiacs to interpose themselves between harpoon and whale, in protest of the slaughter. But the procedure became *too* standard— being practiced at times and in situations that actually called for different tactics. I would be involved personally in such an operation one more time when we confronted Soviet whalers in 1976. I was first mate aboard the converted Canadian minesweeper *James Bay* in *Greenpeace VII*, the foundation's second expedition to save whales, this time in the Pacific, north of Hawaii.

Like so many others who have been drawn irresistibly to the sea, I was born a long way from it. The first five years of my life were spent in inland Canada—amid the Great Lakes, true, but many miles from either of the oceans on whose shores I was to live and on whose waters I was to spend so many years.

I was born December 2, 1950, the first of what would eventually be a family of six children (four boys and two girls), in Toronto, Ontario, Canada. It was the time of the Korean War, and my father, who was then twenty-two years of age, soon afterward was soldiering in Korea with the Canadian Blackwatch Regiment. My father,

Anthony Joseph Watson, is a French-Canadian from Gaspé, his roots there going back many generations despite his English name. His dialect is Acadian, the French patois spoken by those tough and resourceful people who had made their way to Canada because of religious and cultural persecution in Europe. They had settled largely in Nova Scotia and flowed down the east coast of the United States to southern Louisiana. There, as immortalized in Henry Wadsworth Longfellow's epic poem "Evangeline," they declared they had found *Acadia*, the promised land, and built new homes among the rivers and bayous and forests that, to this day, are known as "the Evangeline country."

The English strain springs from another war, the French and Indian, from 1754 to 1760, involving France and England in what is now southeastern and central Canada and the northeastern and upper central United States. Many of the British soldiers who fought under General James Wolfe stayed on after his death in 1759 and married French women among the settler families in Quebec, then called New France. That is how the first Watson in our family started out in Canada, but it is the only English name on my father's side.

My father's mother was of French extraction. Born Angela Dorion, she was still relatively young when she died of complications arising from the birth of her thirteenth child. Her husband and my paternal grandfather, Joseph Watson, a devout Roman Catholic who speaks no English, never remarried. As of this writing, he is farming in New Brunswick on Canada's east coast. I was named after his brother Paul, who was serving as a torpedo boat commander in the Canadian Navy when he was killed in World War II.

My father was still trying to learn English at the time

he met my mother in Toronto. Childbirth complications were involved in her death, too. After bearing six children, Annamarie Larsen Watson lost her seventh child through miscarriage and then succumbed herself. That was in 1963, when I was not quite thirteen years old. Losing one's mother is a devastating blow at any age, but particularly for a boy approaching adolescence who is the oldest of six children thus orphaned. Until then, I had led what seemed to be an idyllic existence. My mother's death tore us all apart, my father as well as his young and uncomprehending offspring. Without my mother's gentle buffering, it seemed my father and I, as the oldest, collided on one issue or another almost every day.

My father had been away so much that our behavior toward each other was often strained. I felt closer to my mother's father, Otto Larsen, with whom we lived in Toronto while my father was in the Blackwatch in Korea. Grandfather Larsen was then an art professor at the University of Toronto and spent much of his time at the Riverdale Zoo, painting pictures of the animals. I accompanied him frequently and soon absorbed a formidable amount of knowledge about the animals, plus a growing affinity for them. I got to know all of them, and the love seeded then has flourished ever since. My childish hope was to be a scientist in a discipline oriented somehow toward caring for animals.

Grandfather Larsen had a colorful past. He had been asked to leave his native Denmark in 1887— "exiled for political reasons," he said, and that was about all I ever got out of him on the subject. He became, in turn, a professional prizefighter, a soldier of fortune who fought under Teddy Roosevelt with the Rough Riders in the Spanish-American War, a lumberjack in

Oregon, and a fisherman in Washington. Eventually, he settled in Toronto, where he married at the age of sixty-two. By that time, thanks mostly to his schooling in Austria and Germany, he had acquired knowledge of thirteen languages. He fathered three children: my mother, the second one, was born when he was sixty-four. My grandmother, Doris Clark Larsen, was eighteen years of age when she entered upon the marriage, arranged by her mother in the Old World fashion. Grandfather Larsen, ever nonconformist, divorced his young wife when he was sixty-nine, saying simply, "I do not want to be married any more." He lived and painted in Toronto until his death at the age of ninety-six.

There were sad goodbyes when we moved from Grandfather Larsen's home in 1955 after my father came back from Korea. But, in truth, for a boy not yet five years old, it was an even exchange of fantasy settings: the wonders of the Riverdale Zoo for the wonders of St. Andrews-by-the-Sea in southernmost New Brunswick. The fishing village, noted for its lobsters, sits on a point jutting into Passamaquoddy Bay at the mouth of the St. Croix River that forms the border between Canada and the United States—New Brunswick on the east bank and the State of Maine on the west. Directly to the south lies Campobello Island, where Franklin D. Roosevelt used to summer. Farther out, to the east and south, are the Bay of Fundy, Nova Scotia, and the great Atlantic Ocean itself.

The Canadian government's marine biology station in St. Andrews-by-the-Sea drew me like a magnet. Its primary tasks included studies of the bay's tidal power and of marine life generally. I was out fishing almost every day from our arrival in 1955 until we moved to London, Ontario, in 1964—after my mother's death the year before—and I spent a lot of time at the marine biology station. I even had a volunteer job there when I was eleven, which helped set the course that led to my activist protests against nuclear testing in 1971 and, by extension, most of my other expeditions.

It is not uncommon for boys to run away from home. In my case, I did not so much run away as drift away. I left my father's house in London, Ontario, at first to work in Montreal, Quebec, as a tour guide at Expo 67, Canada's international fair; I found that I not only could support myself while living alone but that I also liked it. As the Expo 67 work played out, I went west to Vancouver, British Columbia, "riding the rails" as a sixteen-year-old hobo aboard the Canadian National Railway's boxcars.

My first sight of the Pacific Ocean and my first taste of its tangy, salt air decided me. They were full confirmation of my lingering desire to go to sea. To my surprise, becoming a merchant seaman was simplicity itself. Advised by a friend, David Sellers, who would later captain my whaler-ramming boat, the *Sea Shepherd*, and armed with a brand-new Canadian passport, I signed up at the Norwegian Consulate in Vancouver as a deckboy on the motorship *Bris*. She was a 35,000-ton bulk carrier, registered in Oslo and manifested for the Pacific and Indian Ocean trade. The year was 1968, and I was seventeen and free, big and strong, and I could feel vitality surging through my very marrow.

My love affair with the sea and sailing continues to this day, and probably always will be a part of me. From that first day in Vancouver, there has never been anything else for me quite like the feel of a ship making its way through blue water. At times, it seems the sea and the air and the sky all come together as one, and for the sole purpose of creating that voyage. Those are the good times, and they help offset the hardships of hauling hawsers in sore hands, polishing brightwork, chipping paint, and swabbing decks. Even in the hard work, at sea there is a special satisfaction and contentment that I have never found in similar work ashore.

From Vancouver, the *Bris* went to Iran, where we delivered paper, sulphur, and potash, and on to Mozambique, South Africa, Japan, Malaysia, and the Philippines. My young life nearly came to an end in Mozambique. In all innocence, and perhaps also trying to be "one of the boys," I became embroiled in a barroom brawl in which I was lucky not to be killed. Afterward, I drank too much and woke up in the jungle, some twenty miles from port, with no money and a Portuguese cab driver and two huge Zulus insisting I owed them money. I asked no questions, and, when taken back to the ship, borrowed money and paid off everybody. I did not drink anything alcoholic for the next year and a half.

During this period, as the 1960s became the 1970s, I was spending more time on environmental protection and working especially with the Don't Make a Wave Committee. It had been formed in late 1969 by three Vancouver Quakers who were also active in the conservationist Sierra Club—James Bohlen, Paul Coté, and Irving Stowe. Their primary aim was to interfere with and, if possible, halt underground United States nuclear tests as scheduled for the following two years in the National Wildlife Refuge at Amchitka in the Aleutian Islands of the Northern Pacific. The name of the organization came from a sign used in a demonstration protesting that tests might trigger a tidal wave such as one that had battered North America's West Coast in

1964 after undersea earthquakes. This Canadian movement was boosted by the *Earth Day* celebration on April 22, 1970, when millions of people in the United States demonstrated against pollution; thereafter, the color green was adopted everywhere as the symbol of life and growth. As we ended one of our Don't Make a Wave meetings, somebody, as usual, made a capital V-sign with two fingers and said, "Peace!" Somebody else, thinking environmentally, said, "Make it a green peace!" Everybody agreed that "Greenpeace" had a nice ring to it and would make a good name for the Amchitka expedition then under consideration. By 1972, we had become so used to the name that we had begun calling our organization the "Greenpeace Foundation." When we made it official that year, I was one of the founders.

Greenpeace I, the first expedition, was designed to put a boatload of protesters in the nuclear test area in order to present authorities with the choice of either calling off the 1971 test explosion or killing the protesters. It was made aboard the *Phyllis Cormack*, the same halibut-seiner that we were to use in the confrontation with the Soviet whalers off San Francisco in 1975. The first expedition managed to create considerable publicity reflecting negatively on the nuclear tests, but it was ultimately aborted; crew members inadvertently violated United States customs laws by going ashore on United States territory without proper credentials.

Much to my chagrin, I was not able to go along on that trip. I vowed to make the next one, and, in the meantime, filled my hours, when I was not working to make a living, with studies and activities centering on conservation—especially those issues dealing with sea mammals. I was an active member of the Society for Pollution and Environmental Control, wrote freelance for *Georgia Straight*, a Vancouver weekly, and studied linguistics and communication (with a special interest in interspecies communication) at Simon Fraser University.

We at Greenpeace were anxious not to let our protests against nuclear testing collapse because of technicalities that stymied picketing at sea aboard the *Phyllis Cormack*. The *Edgewater Fortune*, which had been a Canadian Navy minesweeper, was hired as a relief ship for the *Phyllis Cormack*. She was a much bigger, faster vessel, and she was designated, in punnish whimsy, the *Greenpeace Too*.

I was determined not to be left behind the second time.

3

The Struggle Begins

JOHN WAYNE WAS A BIG HELP TO US, although that was not the way he had planned it. The movie star, idol of millions, actually loathed everything we were trying to do in those closing months of 1971. But, as often happens, by opposing us with his typical vigor, he gave our fund-raising efforts such a boost that we were able to go over the top and launch the expedition he heartily wanted stopped.

Wayne, following his custom, showed up in Victoria aboard his yacht (naturally enough, for him, a converted U.S. Navy minesweeper) to go fishing near Campbell River. His timing was perfect. He had sailed smack into a beehive of activity: we had already sent the *Phyllis Cormack* to the United States nuclear testing grounds as *Greenpeace I* and we were just launching concerted fund-raising to charter the *Edgewater Fortune* as a relief vessel called *Greenpeace Too.*

Canadian news reporters caught Wayne aboard his yacht, shared a drink or two with him, and then put the question: What did he think about the Canadian protests seeking to block the American tests?

Wayne puckered his eyebrows, looked up through them and said, "Canadian and Japanese concern over the Amchitka tests is a lot of crap. We need that bomb to stop the Commies. So just mind your own goddam business."

When that news flashed across Canada, the money came pouring in. Not only those Canadians who had been active environmentalists against pollution sent in their money; funds came also from those who were more or less neutral or uninformed on emerging environmentalist issues but still nationalistic enough to resent Wayne or anybody else talking down to them. Feelings ran so high that Air Canada announced it was banning John Wayne movies from its flights.

Like his movie persona, though, Wayne pushed on. He took his yacht to the north, saying he was hunting the protesters to "teach 'em a lesson," and, while none of us ever ran across him on the water, we did happen to pick up his trail. We met two of Wayne's crewmen in a bar in Sand Point, Alaska. They welcomed us as old friends. They said they had jumped ship.

The publicity stirred up by Wayne was also a boon for Pierre Berton, Canada's most prolific writer. All the hoopla helped him complete a pet project that surely belongs in the *Guinness Book of Records*. This involved a telegram addressed to United States President Nixon, protesting against the nuclear tests. Every Canadian who sent in at least a dime had his or her name inscribed on it. The telegram was two miles long, I understand, and was rolled into the White House aboard a wheelbarrow. President Nixon took no official notice of the telegram.

We hoped that if we could stir up the Canadian people and their government to the point of protest, it might persuade the Americans not to cause further radioactive pollution. We meant it only in a neighborly way, but we were sure we were right. In Washington, where the Senate Foreign Relations Committee discussed calling off the tests right up to the day before the Amchitka blast, and where the U.S. Supreme Court kept considering and ruling on the issue, too, we knew we had a sensitive and heedful audience.

Only about a dozen volunteers comprised the crew of the *Phyllis Cormack*, which had already been in Alaskan waters some two months, but we sailed as *Greenpeace Too* aboard the *Edgewater Fortune* some thirty strong. Our skipper was Hank Johansen, and our crew ranged from young people like me to a number in middle-age, such as Will James, our navigator. He was one of the more qualified people aboard, a member of an old Pennsylvania family, a World War II officer in the U.S. Navy, and a former Atomic Energy Commission scientist. He had just accepted a position on the faculty of Simon Fraser University, where I was enrolled in a linguistics course, and was fast becoming an enthusiastic Canadian. We also had heavy news media representation aboard, for obvious reasons: the whole point of our jaunt was to stir up publicity.

The *Edgewater Fortune,* built for the Canadian Navy in 1956, was sleek and graceful, 154 feet long, and capable of twenty-two knots. As a minesweeper, she had a hull that was mostly wood and aluminum so as to avoid attracting to her most vulnerable parts the magnetically detonated mines she was designed to collect. This made her lighter than an all-steel vessel of the same displacement, but, together with her narrow beam, it also made her more prone to pitching and rolling. Her mostly amateur crew was violently seasick on the voyage from Vancouver to Juneau (through a storm) and across the Gulf of Alaska—only to learn one day out of Amchitka that the AEC had detonated its H-device ahead of schedule.

The most disappointed among us on that Saturday, November 6, 1971, were the four who had been aboard the *Phyllis Cormack* and had switched over to the *Edgewater Fortune* for the final run at Amchitka: David Birmingham, Robert Cummings, Rod Marining, and Terry Simmons. We were all pretty gloomy, though, as we turned and headed back to Sand Point, Alaska, where we had rendezvoused earlier with the *Phyllis Cormack* and formally relieved her.

This time, the weather was worse than usual, and we made a dramatic return to Sand Point. Coming up hard on the pier in the rough water, we collided with a resounding bang. The women in the nearby crab cannery came out screaming and on the run. They told us later they thought that there had been an earthquake, such as the one they had experienced a few years earlier, or that perhaps another atomic device had gone off, a little closer than it was supposed to.

We laughed, but even those of us who were not suffering *mal de mer* saw little in our situation to be happy about. We felt, as we spent a day in Sand Point to prepare our homeward trip, that we had failed. It was not until we got back to Vancouver that we began to think that maybe we had accomplished more than we realized. For one thing, never before had Canada come together in a protest so vigorously expressed. Canadians were united in their indignation at being brushed aside, at not being consulted before the tests were ordered, and so were the Alaskans. For another thing, the United States cancelled its planned explosion of a second device, in the 10-megaton range, and we could not help wondering whether the commotion we had kicked up might have contributed somewhat to that decision. The AEC officials probably believed that, unless we were arrested, some of us intended to be sitting on the ground under which that explosive was to be detonated. And that was exactly right.

Looking back now, it may seem that some of our demonstrations were extreme, that we were overdoing things a bit, unlimbering a field gun to kill a gnat. Perhaps so. But it was not easy then to compete against the John Waynes of the world. And, it might be added, what we did do seemed to work.

These first expeditions were followed up in 1972 and 1973 by David McTaggart's *Greenpeace III* and *Greenpeace IV* aboard his sailing vessel, the *Vega*, against French nuclear testing in the air over Mururoa Atoll in the South Pacific. During those two years, along with others, I helped support these expeditions with publicity and fund-raising back in Vancouver. I also pursued my work at sea—moving now from oiler aboard the *Edgewater Fortune* to able seaman on the Swedish *Jarl R. Trapp*, making trips to Malaysia and Iran, and aboard a yacht out of Brindisi in Italy. I continued to do freelance writing as well for the Vancouver weekly, *Georgia Straight*. But my primary interest was in backing such efforts as McTaggart's. McTaggart, a Canadian, when ordered in 1972 by the French to leave their test area, refused and claimed the right of freedom of the seas in international waters. The French responded by having a minesweeper (one given to France by the Canadian government, incidentally) ram the *Vega* and leave her to the mercies of the sea. McTaggart and his crew limped to haven in New Zealand. But they were back in 1973, practiced this time in the art of dodging minesweepers. A French commando unit stormed aboard and gave McTaggart a gang beating that robbed him of the sight of his left eye. His lawsuits against the French government, financed in part by the sale of the *Vega* and in part by fund-raising for him in Canada, cost more than $150,000. He won in each case in the Paris courts, but awards fell short of costs, and it is not clear whether he will ever be able to collect from the French government, regardless of what the courts decided.

The chance to avenge McTaggart came in late 1973 with the arrival in Vancouver of two French Navy ships on a goodwill visit. These were the helicopter carrier *Jeanne d'Arc* and her escort vessel, the *Victor Schroeder*.

As part of our demonstration, I took the wheel of Bob Hunter's fifteen-foot fishing boat, a rather decrepit number, and, with a few people aboard and a lot of anti-nuclear signs, lit out across the harbor just as the *Jeanne d'Arc* headed out at the end of her visit. Our engine broke down. By the time I had it going again, we had missed the *Jeanne d'Arc*.

But the *Victor Schroeder* was coming along behind her. At the helm, I put our little boat right in front of the *Victor Schroeder* and headed straight for her. It was a David and Goliath situation. In the choppy water, we were so small that we might not even be seen. From where we were, the destroyer escort looked gigantic. And it was getting bigger and bigger as we resolutely closed the distance.

The Coast Guard and the Harbor Police had already figured out what we were up to, and they came at us in their speedy boats from either side. So intent were they to head us off that they almost ran into each other. Only the most skillful helmsmanship by both vessels at the last moment avoided a collision.

It was quite a tableau, almost like a water ballet. While the Coast Guard and Harbor Police boats made their sweeping circles to start another run at us, I held steady for the *Victor Schroeder*. She changed course to avoid me. I headed for her again, and again she changed course. A third time, I aimed straight at her bow, and this time there was no room for her to maneuver out of our way. In the last few feet, as the bow came up like some monstrous axe blade, I pushed the wheel to starboard and we bounced over the bow wash and raced alongside the big vessel. She plowed past us some ten feet away.

Looking up, we could see the French sailors on deck standing rigidly at attention, prepared to salute as they passed under the Lion's Gate Bridge. Some of them broke ranks and leaned over the railing, cheering. Officers came up and pushed and shouted at them, but the cheering went on.

At the bridge, we had planned a surprise. As the ship passed under, an enormous banner made up of about twenty bedsheets stitched together was unfurled from the bridge's railing. On it, in great letters, was the legend, MURUROA, MON AMOUR! We hoped the French would appreciate the connection between their Mururoa Atoll test explosion and the anti-nuclear film, *Hiroshima, Mon Amour,* which had made such an impression on people around the world that we often used it as a kind of slogan for anti-nuclear activities.

Our confederates on the bridge also dumped buckets of mushrooms and marshmallows on the *Victor Schroeder*, to symbolize atomic explosions. The mushroom/marshmallow people were arrested, and I heard later that some of the French sailors were punished, too. But, in a world in which small victories sometimes loom large if they come when you need them, it was, all in all, a very satisfying day.

Since then, in my travels around the world, I have

run into French sailors who, upon hearing I am from Vancouver, start telling me this story. Sometimes I acknowledge my role in it, and sometimes discretion suggests that I keep quiet. But, overwhelmingly, those French sailors are laughing at themselves and the human condition whenever they remember the day they were showered with mushrooms and marshmallows at the bridge in Canada.

Life was not always so hectic for me at this time. There were quiet, contemplative moments, too. I was doing landscape work at Stanley Park, and I was writing and reading and thinking about where everything was going. One of the books I read was *Bury My Heart at Wounded Knee* by Dee Brown. As I read about the repeated injustices visited upon the North American Indians since the coming of the white man, I could hardly believe what I was reading. And yet, I knew it was all true.

"I ought to go down there and do something," I said to myself. But I had no idea what that could be.

Then, on February 28, 1973, I read in the newspaper that, on the day before, some two hundred members of the American Indian Movement had seized the trading post and church at Wounded Knee.

That was it. I had to go.

4

Wounded Knee

DAVID GARRICK AND I JUMPED INTO an old truck and took off for South Dakota. If somebody had been awarding blue ribbons for naïveté, we would have been in a dead heat for them, David and I. We had a vague idea about where South Dakota was and we knew from the newspapers and television and radio accounts that Wounded Knee was in South Dakota. The rest we left to Providence and the kindness of strangers who, we assumed, would help show us the way.

I was very happy to have somebody my own age along, and I was particularly glad that it was somebody with whom I had grown comfortable. David Garrick and I had already become good friends. We would share many adventures, in addition to the incredible experience awaiting us at Wounded Knee, and it was always good to know David was near. He was totally dependable.

David's family had been associated with the theater for many generations, tracing its lineage, in fact, to the celebrated English actor, playwright, and theatrical producer of the eighteenth century, David Garrick, for whom David was named. That Garrick, friend and associate of Dr. Samuel Johnson, and one of history's most celebrated Shakespeareans (his *Hamlet*, I have been told, is considered unsurpassed to this day, on the basis of contemporary accounts), exerted a magical influence on the males of the family through the generations, so that, by tradition, they entered the theater. But not my friend David. He chose journalism, instead.

David shared my great love for animals and the environment. However, where I tended to work on the practical level, seeking to effect conservation through organization and demonstration, David depended upon instinct and a rather mystical sense of what would work for the cause and what would not. As part of his rebuking to the world for its readiness to sacrifice natural beauty to commercial gain, and also, I suspect, to assert his indepedence, he changed his name to the rather fanciful "Walrus Oakenbough." That was the only name he would answer to for a long time, and the name he used in bylines on his stories about our adventures. It was a mild eccentricity, and I had no problems with it whatsoever. He eventually tired of the pseudonym and returned to "David Garrick."

As David and I drove toward South Dakota from Vancouver, we reviewed our meager knowledge of Wounded Knee. The massacre at Wounded Knee of December 29, 1890, was an event fixed more clearly in our heads than whatever was happening there in 1973. We knew, for instance, that the white man's history called Wounded Knee a battle—indeed, it is recorded as the "last major conflict between Indians and U.S. troops." Yet, from *Bury My Heart at Wounded Knee* and from American Indian sources, we knew that it was, purely and simply, a wipe-out: more than two hundred Indian men, women, and children killed, only twenty-nine soldiers dead (and some of the soldiers were believed killed accidentally by their cohorts).

Now, what David and I were driving toward was a highly volatile situation involving Indians who felt that they could no longer go along with the injustices still prevailing despite the passage of time and recent advances in civil rights. The Indian insurgents had taken over the Oglala Sioux Reservation at Wounded Knee and set up their headquarters in the reservation's trading post and church. They were demanding a full-scale investigation by the United States Senate of the government's treatment of Indians, plus hearings before the Senate Foreign Relations Committee on treaties made with the Indians over the two centuries since creation of the United States of America.

Our plan, if it could be called that, was to offer ourselves for service, any service, at Wounded Knee. I knew that the Oglala Sioux had fought to save the buffalo; for David Garrick and me, that was enough.

David had seen the Great Plains of the middle United States before, but it was all strange territory to me. We came into South Dakota from the west, driving through great heaps of snow covering the state's famous short-stubble grazing land. We pulled into Shannon County in the southwestern corner of the state and then charged into Pine Ridge Reservation. I leaned out of the window of our truck cab and shouted at a group of men:

"Where's Wounded Knee?"

They waved us on, and, within a very few minutes, we ran into an FBI line. The Federal Bureau of Investigation people there arrested us immediately. We were booked: crime on an Indian reservation. Specifically, our crime was: possession of a deadly weapon—that is, the woodman's axe in the back of the truck). They locked us up for eight hours and then let us go.

Rain was coming down in sheets as we got back in our truck and pulled out of wherever we were. We were still fumbling for Wounded Knee and getting no directional help from anybody, least of all our FBI friends. Blinded and confused by the heavy rain, and far too anxious to join the beleaguered Indians at Wounded Knee, we ran off the road and into a ditch. We sat there for a few minutes, wondering what next to do.

Suddenly, a half dozen Indians materialized and offered to give us a helping hand. With their aid we got back on the road. They invited us to a house nearby that we could not even see through the downpour. There, over a beer, we got our first inkling of the situation.

They told us we were in a place called Calico. Soldiers were all around us, they said, and moved about in a seemingly endless number of armored personnel carriers, which they parked when not in use among the snow-covered patches of underbrush. When we went out to see for ourselves, we found the report absolutely true. The place looked as though it were under military siege, which indeed it was, as we soon found out.

David and I argued over strategy for getting past all those guards and into Wounded Knee. He was counseling patience and a waiting game. I wanted to get in quickly. We decided we could not agree, and so we chose to split up, with a vague notion of getting together again whenever David felt the time was right for him to press on.

David took the wheel of the truck and headed along a road that the Indians said would take us into Wounded Knee. When we calculated we were about twenty miles away from it, David slowed down and we checked around as best we could to make sure nobody was watching. I jumped off the back of the truck and into a snowbank. I lay there for a while, listening intently for some sign of having been discovered, and then I started overland.

The first ten or fifteen miles were not so bad, although I seemed to be forever falling into snow-hidden ravines up to my chin and having to flail my way out of them. When I found myself close to the FBI lines, I would attach tumbleweed and branches to my sweater and crawl past. I kept on plowing ahead like that, always trying to keep on a northerly course and to stay close to the highway so that I would not get lost completely.

In what seemed to me to be an incredibly short time, I realized the sun was coming up. I relaxed, feeling that I had successfully negotiated the FBI and military checkpoints. Wounded Knee *had to be* somewhere nearby. Despite my lack of experience in such wide-open country and despite all the snow cover, I gloated— I had made it, or I soon would.

It was at this point that I went over a hill and walked into a couple of armored personnel carriers surrounded by about a dozen FBI people.

I don't know how many women the FBI has among its agents these days. But I hope all of them are not as tough as the one who now turned her attention to me. She looked me over, head to toe, in a manner that I have seen a full-grown eagle eye his latest prospective meal.

"Where are you going?"

"Oh-ah," I said. "Well . . . um . . . I was just looking for Wounded Knee. Is it this way?"

"O-o-kay," she said. "Just hold it right there!"

I figured the only thing to do was to start talking as fast as I could and hope that my brain would kick into gear and come up with something to say. I told her I was a journalist on assignment from the Vancouver *Sun* to cover events at Wounded Knee. It did no good.

She put me in an FBI staff car, which took me all the way back to Pine Ridge. There, I was charged again, with something like being an alien in the United States during a state of emergency, and ordered to get out of the country within twenty-four hours.

At the office of the Bureau of Indian Affairs in Pine Ridge, as I wandered about and tried to think of what to do next, I noticed a line of people shuffling up to a desk. It dawned on me that this might be my salvation. I stepped into the line, and, when I had reached the head of it, I said in a firm voice, with as much authority as I could muster,

"Vancouver *Sun!*"

The bored bureaucrat on the other side of the desk handed over a press pass without asking me for identification, or even looking up. I fell in with a reporter who said he was from Omaha, Nebraska, and offered me a ride to Wounded Knee. I accepted gladly, and we headed for the next stop—one of the areas at which FBI agents and United States marshals were checking press passes and clearing news media personnel for entry into Wounded Knee, which the government had surrounded but which was in the hands of the Indians. I figured turnabout was fair play, and so I tipped my new acquaintance (which probably improved my cover as a reporter):

"Don't go over there. That's FBI. They'll hassle us for hours. Go over here, to the U.S. marshals. No sweat."

That proved exactly right, and, in a very little while, we were in Wounded Knee. I thanked my Nebraska colleague, bade him goodbye, and went directly to the security building maintained by the leaders of the dissident Indians. I reported who I was and why I was there, and then I called the Vancouver *Sun* and told the editor what I had done. He was infuriated by my having represented myself as one of his paper's reporters, but, after a while, he calmed down, and, despite the liberties I had taken, he seemed genuinely glad that he would have someone on the scene to telephone in eyewitness accounts of a very dramatic, developing story. As it turned out, I was able to call the paper every day and report what was going on, supplying the *Sun* with fresh, inside information for every edition.

At the American Indian Movement headquarters in Wounded Knee, I identified myself once more—making no mention of any connection with the Vancouver *Sun,* of course—and asked how I could help. Did I know enough to be a medic? Sure. I was handed a big bag of Kotex pads, and I knew immediately the leadership expected a firefight. Ever since World War I, the combat-ready always stock up on these highly absorbent bandages, for there is no better way to staunch the flow of blood from gunshot wounds.

David Garrick, meanwhile, had tired of trying to finesse his way into Wounded Knee. After about three or four days of waiting around, he decided to slip into the community under cover of darkness, pretty much the same as he had seen me go at it. David and five Indians who were members of the American Indian Movement started hiking from Pine Ridge as soon as nightfall came, and it was not until they had almost made it that they were discovered by patrolling United States marshals.

The patrol opened fire. David and his five friends dove for cover and started crawling in all directions.

Three of them simply disappeared in the night, amid a hail of tracer bullets. David and two others happened to crawl in the right direction and made it safely to the outer perimeter.

At AIM headquarters in Wounded Knee, we heard the shooting and we could tell by the tracers the general area of the shooting. We held a quick council and decided some people friendly to us were trying to infiltrate the FBI and United States marshals' lines, and it behooved us to help them. We sent a patrol of our own out, mostly sharpshooters who had learned weaponry and infantry tactics in the United States military in Vietnam, and ordered it to give cover to whoever was under attack, engaging anybody shooting at them.

I was astonished to see David Garrick among the three bedraggled-looking men who managed to slip into our camp that night. I was overjoyed, too, and grateful for his good luck. His resourcefulness was no surprise, though.

David joined me as a medic. Our first assignments dealt with treating children, not for gunshot wounds but for the ravages of filth and neglect. I had never before seen so many boils to be lanced. And then, every night (I never did know who would start it, or how) the fireworks would go on. The American Indian Movement taped this "show" one night and later counted the shots recorded—twenty thousand rounds expended in a single night. Parachute flares kept the night skies lit up like daylight. The FBI burned about three miles of grass all around after the snows melted away and things struggled to grow again. The trees went, too. We estimated there were five hundred United States marshals on hand, together with five hundred FBI agents, five hundred members of the U.S. Army's 82nd Airborne

Division, and about sixty armored personnel carriers. Tracer bullets criss-crossed the skies every night in a continual display. It got to such a point that we did not even bother to duck.

Amazingly, there were only two killed during the seventy-one days that the militants held the village, from February 28 to May 8, and both of them were Indians. Only six were wounded, five Indians and one United States marshal, who was left paralyzed.

In some ways, it seemed to me, the Oglala Sioux had come full circle. From the massacre at Wounded Knee in 1890, followed by decades of wretchedness as virtual wards of the government, mired in poverty, sickness, and alcoholism, they had lashed out once more at Wounded Knee. But they were no better off than before. Once again, there were government promises and government rhetoric, and once again no follow-through. When the media lights went off, the investigations promised in the U.S. Congress faded to black, too.

Yet, there was this to reckon with: Wounded Knee 1890 had signaled the Indians that they had to adapt to the white man's ways or vanish. Wounded Knee 1973 proved that they had done neither. Their numbers had tripled since 1890, when the Indian population was only 250,000, and they had showed that they might have to be dealt with again and again until justice was done.

There was this, too, from the ashes of Wounded Knee: there was evidence that Crazy Horse and Red Cloud and all the other great Oglala Sioux leaders of the last century were no greater than the men and women in leadership roles today. Under terrible pressures, Dennis Banks and Leonard Crow Dog and all the others proved themselves true leaders, as resourceful as their predecessors, and much, much more educated. The American Indians learned that they still produce great leaders, fully qualified to lead as the times demand.

By May 8 there was no longer anything left to defend in Wounded Knee. The Indians had made their point, anyway. Leonard Crow Dog told a council he had had a vision in which all the people had placed their weapons in a teepee and an eagle had flown low over it. This was interpreted as a sign that the time had come to put away force and negotiate for fair treatment. Wounded Knee was evacuated. The soldiers and the marshals and the G-men and G-women packed up their weapons and armored personnel carriers and went home. It is not a good page in United States history, but a proud one for American Indians.

David and I were given a special honor by the Oglala Sioux. Leonard Crow Dog and Wallace Black Elk, as medicine men of the people at Wounded Knee, initiated us into the Oglala Sioux tribe as full-fledged members even though we were not Oglala Sioux by birth and by blood. In separate ceremonies inside the sacred sweat lodge at Wounded Knee, we acquired new names, David becoming Two Deer Lone Eagle and I assuming the name of Grey Wolf Clear Water.

When we returned to Vancouver, we both knew we would never be the same again. Indians are a spiritual people in general, and it is difficult to be around them without feeling something of that creeping under your skin and into your bones. But the practical side of me resisted total surrender, even as I experienced events that I could not explain except in mystical terms. Further, shared danger always draws people closer, and the risks we had taken at Wounded Knee knitted me into the Oglala Sioux as fully as the solemn ceremony conducted by Wallace Black Elk, acting for himself and Leonard Crow Dog as tribal leaders as well as on behalf of all Oglala Sioux. Even without my membership in the tribe now, even without my tribal name, I felt like an Oglala Sioux, and I always would, from that time forward.

Back in Vancouver, I served briefly aboard the Canadian Coast Guard weather ship, the *Vancouver*, before going abroad again—for yacht work in Rhodes, Greece, and as a lecturer on North American Indians for the Anglo-American studies program at the University of Paris. In 1974, I was an able seaman aboard the Canadian Coast Guard supply ship *Camsell* and a rescue officer on the Canadian Coast Guard's search and rescue hovercraft at Vancouver International Airport. I also put in another semester of linguistics and communication studies at Simon Fraser University.

By 1975, at the age of twenty-four, I felt the die had been cast in my life. There never had been any doubt in my mind that I would work for conservation and the protection of the environment. I knew that my inclinations were toward specifics—which is to say, animals. But now I also knew that I would concentrate on animals of the sea. This conviction solidified after my induction into the Oglala Sioux just before David Garrick and I left Wounded Knee.

The Indians of North America believe generally that one can be closer to his inner spirit, more at peace with himself and the universe, by undergoing unusual changes in his physical environment. Sometimes, this involves physical deprivation, even suffering. At such times, the experience may produce hallucinations that are somewhere between a dream and a vision. With the

Oglala Sioux and some other tribes, this is done by having the person involved enter a "sweat lodge," as David and I did individually, under tightly controlled conditions. The lodge is a small enclosure, made of buffalo hide and sticks. It is heated to an intense degree. The man enters nude, and, in a short while, the extreme heat and the loss of oxygen in the small space induces anoxia, and the hallucinatory (or visionary, as you see it) state generally follows.

What happened to me was that I saw a huge buffalo, the great animal that is to the Great Plains of North America what the elephant is to Africa and the whale is to the world's oceans. The buffalo seemed to talk to me as I lay sweating and gasping for air inside the incredibly hot lodge. It seemed to say that I should look to the whales, that I should not dissipate my energies on the full range of animal life, but that I should concentrate on the mammals of the sea, especially whales.

I am sure there are simple physical and psychological laws to explain what happened to me inside that enclosure of buffalo hides and sticks. If it was a dream it was the most vividly realistic dream I had ever had. In any case, it brought my whole life into focus, in the sense that I knew exactly what I meant to do with myself from then on.

5

The Labrador Front

Our 1975 confrontation in the pacific with the Soviet whalers was an enormous propaganda success, particularly on television, and we were all delighted with the results. But, as we jumped to the dock from the *Phyllis Cormack,* our first problem was raising money once again—to pay off an indebtedness of something like $48,000, all told.

We did it the usual way, by rattling tin cans in front of people on downtown streets, holding huge musical concerts, and doing everything else we could think of. I represented Greenpeace in the 1975 National Whale Symposium at the University of Indiana in Bloomington, where groups such as ours hoped to effect an international ban on the killing of whales. In the same year, I became a founder and editor of the *Greenpeace Chronicles,* the foundation's colorful and sprightly (I hoped) quarterly newsletter. About this time, too, David Garrick and I began to work up a bold scheme to call world attention to the atrocities being committed (with the official blessing of the Canadian government) against harp seals in Newfoundland.

Like all seals, the harp seals of the Western Atlantic Ocean have few natural enemies, and their newborn pups do not flee at the sight of man. In the water, seals move with a grace that is sheer poetry, but, like other species out of their element, they are less than agile when flopping about on land, and they would have trouble escaping hunters even if they tried. Thus, it is an overstatement to call the annual seal hunt a "hunt," for there is no need to hunt—the seals are simply there, waiting in all innocence for whatever occurs.

Every year, in March, so-called hunters from Canada and Norway bash in the heads of tens of thousands of these newborns. They go out on the ice floes off Newfoundland called the Labrador Front and kill them (and their mothers, too, if they resist or otherwise get in the way) for one purpose: to acquire their white pelts for the lucrative fur industry. The seals, only a few weeks old, are generally not used for foot. Their skinned bodies are left on the ice—a horrifying sight. At first glance they look human.

The harp seal (*Pagophilus groenlandicus*) draws its common name from the harp-shaped black mark on its silvery back. It bears one infant at a time. The pup, only fifteen pounds at birth, lacks the blubber that will insulate it against the bitter cold of its environment when maturity is reached, and that is primarily why the coat is white—to draw in the sun's warming rays. The pup thrives on its mother's rich milk, and, in three weeks, weighs a hundred pounds. As blubber comes, the white darkens to what is called a "beater" pelt.

Baby harp seals are among the most appealing of nature's creatures. Conservationist Brian Davies, who has spent the better part of the past two decades fighting for the preservation of seals, once wrote the following description of his first meeting, in 1965, with a "whitecoat":

"The eyes—dark and inquisitive—captivated me

first. Then my eyes were drawn to a twitching black button of a nose with dark, stiff whiskers jutting to each side. The inch-long hair that covered the young animal looked like the white puff of a dandelion. And then, as I stared, all but the eyes and nose of the tiny harp seal gradually seemed to disappear as its body blended into the incredible whiteness of the ice. . . ."

One of the most charming anecdotes about the harp seal pup comes to us from Dr. Wilfred T. Grenfell, a medical missionary to Labrador who wrote the following in 1909:

"It had not been easy to convey to the Eskimo mind the meaning of the Oriental (Middle East) similes of the Bible. Thus, the Lamb of God had to be translated *kotik*, or young seal. This animal, with its perfect whiteness as it lies in its cradle of ice, its gentle, helpless nature, and its pathetic innocent eyes, is probably as apt a substitute, however, as Nature offers."

Thanks to the annual seal hunts, the harp seal population in the Western Atlantic is headed for extinction. At the turn of the century, the total number of harp seals in the world was about twenty million. In 1964, the number had fallen to three million. Today, estimates run below one million, and the curve of the trend is down. It does not take an ecologist, or even a mathematician, to recognize that the harp seal, at this rate, will soon be no more. The Canadian government once acknowledged this.

An official commission to study the seal hunt was appointed by Ottawa in 1971. This was in response to heavy objections raised all over the world as a result of campaigns by Cleveland Amory of the Fund for Animals, Brian Davies of the International Fund for Animal Welfare, and a few other conservationists. This committee on seals and sealing was a blue-ribbon panel of Canadian biologists and other wildlife experts. Foes of the seal hunt expected a whitewash, but the committee surprised them with "a definite conclusion based on scientific analyses of available data between 1950 and 1970 . . . that the stock of harp seals has been halved . . . [and] the population trend towards decrease is continuing." The committee recommended sharp cutbacks in the killing quotas—from 245,000 in 1971 to 90,000 in both 1972 and 1973 and 80,000 in 1974, and none at all for at least six years beginning in 1975, except for some limited killings by "native peoples." After that, the committee expected that the herd would have begun to build up its numbers again.

The Canadian government applauded the finding and praised the commission. But it acted only in the Gulf of St. Lawrence, center of most of the publicity. The number to be killed there was reduced, but the total quota for 1974 was set at 160,000—exactly twice the figure recommended by the commission. (Of course, nobody knows for certain how many baby seals actually die. The count covers only the pelts that are "harvested." It is not a total body count. It omits the dead and dying that are always left behind, and the dead among the protesting mothers.)

Thus, despite the commission's good work, the 1974 quota was identical to those of 1972 and 1973. That was the Canadian government's decision despite the findings of its own biologists that the herd would collapse if as many as 125,000 were taken. And this was done even though the sealers could not meet their quota of 245,000 in 1971. They could find and "harvest" only 219,000 baby seals—clear evidence that, unless the hunts eased off or stopped altogether, attrition would wipe out the species.

One excuse trotted out by the Canadian and Norwegian governments was that the harp seals interfere with commercial cod fishing because they eat the cod and also carry a worm that gets into the cod and makes the fish taste unpleasant unless treated with ultrasonic vibrations, an expensive process. However, the facts are that the seals do not feed on cod but on capelin, a noncommercial fish. Further, no conclusive evidence ever has been offered that the seals carry the worms and pass them on to cod. Yet, by solemnly making such statements, these governments give the impression of nobly acting on behalf of their people—better still, their working people.

Yet, in truth, the men who actually go out on the ice and club the baby seals to death get only one dollar from the four to five hundred dollars that each pelt actually brings in the fur market. The seal hunters' annual pay averages only two to three hundred dollars. The big profit goes to commercial interests, which—as reported repeatedly by Lewis Regenstein, executive vice president of the Fund for Animals in Washington, D.C.—are "controlled for the most part by one family," with branches in Halifax, Nova Scotia, and Bergen, Norway. These branches, Regenstein says, are Karlsen Shipping Company of Halifax, owned by Karl Karlsen, and the G. C. Reba Company of Bergen, headed by Christian Reba, thought to have family ties to Karlsen.

Any hope we had of help from the United States government—which, over the years, had taken the lead in imposing bans or sanctions on whaling and pelagic (on the high seas) sealing—seemed unrealistic as we prepared our 1976 campaign. The Americans had their own shame in the Alaskan Pribilof Islands. Each May or so, the northern fur seals (*Callorhinus ursinus*) return to the Pribilofs to spawn and breed. A couple of months later, the resident Aleuts segregate out the "bachelors"—that is, the males without a harem—and slaughter them, usually about 75 percent of the males three and four years old. The United States government claims that the Pribilof herd is now stabilized at about one and a half million, up from 200,000 in 1911, when pelagic killing was legal. Yet, there are many signs that these claims are unfounded and that the herd is in serious trouble. For example, births are down from 438,000 in 1961 to 306,000 in 1970, and the bachelor "harvest" fell from 126,046 in 1961 to 37,500 in recent years. Since one of the seal rookeries was declared a sanctuary, the kill rate has fallen to 26,000 annually.

And so, David Garrick and I pretty much wrote off the United States as a source of official pressure on the governments of Canada and Norway. But we continued to depend upon private Americans for moral and financial support, of course. And, more than anything else, we pressed our research into the harp seal situation, gathering as much evidence as we could to support our case that, unless the killing stopped, the Western Atlantic herd would collapse.

One of the most horrifying aspects is that not all of the babies die with one blow of the club, or the *hak-a-pik,* which is like an axe handle or a skinny baseball bat with a six-inch steel hook at its striking end. Some do not die at all, even after repeated blows. These are then skinned alive, not out of sadism or even cruelty, but because the men are working in the cold and must move fast. During the few days of the "hunt"—which could be compared to loggers hunting trees to cut down—the sealers kill a pup every thirty seconds.

These men, or so the government maintains, do not relish their work, despite the *macho* mystique that surrounds the hunt. But the hunt provides sorely needed employment in a depressed area, at least in this part of the year.

"No one really wants to skin live seals," one man, Sven Hanson, told me in Newfoundland. "These cases are accidents but sometimes you cannot avoid them. It is cold, the wind blows, it starts snowing. You try to get seals, the club freezes in your hand, you aim and miss. You aim again—you hit it, but not too well. You hit three, four times. You are sure it's dead now. So you turn it, open it, and start tearing its skin off. Suddenly it rolls its eyes at you and screams its head off. Yes, it happened to me more than once during a trip. I am not proud of it, but it happened."

Another Norwegian sealer, Eric Nielson, told me, "It's a miserable tragic business. No, I don't like it at all. I think it's the most perverted trade that I have ever been in. I need the money. They pay me money but they cannot make me like what I am doing. This is my last trip. I have not seen any cases of live skinning. You don't need to see it. Sealing is horrible enough without that ultimate perversity. I did see something that you would like to print. One of my shipmates deliberately blinded a mother seal with his gaff. He thought it was great fun to watch the poor thing stumble on the ice. I killed her."

Yet, some men have a far different reaction to this "miserable tragic business." Some share the emotions described by a journalist named Pol Chantraine in the March 30, 1980, Toronto *Sunday Star*. He told about his first hunt two weeks earlier, when the quota had been raised to 180,000 pups. He said a veteran sealer acting as his mentor had led him out among tens of thousands of crying baby seals, and their very cries had aroused within him a "secret desire" to kill them. And then he saw his teacher kill a pup, skin it, reach into the animal's chest cavity and scoop out blood with a cupped hand. He drank the blood straightaway, and then:

"What bewildered me . . . was to see him smear his cheekbones and eyelids with the blood that remained on his hands, carefully, expertly, like a woman applying makeup.

" 'The morning sun is bad for the eyes,' he said, in response to the amazed look on my face. 'It can cause snow-blindness.' "

Chantraine wrote that his mentor explained he had learned this "religious ceremony" as a boy from his father, who had picked it up from the Indians. The man said it was a ritual that made the hunter a "blood brother" to the seal and therefore set the killings to right. He finished by saying as he pointed to a slain seal, "Your turn."

"Despite the disgust I felt at the thought of drinking blood, I dropped to my knees, trying to shut off my senses, scooped up a handful of blood and quickly gulped it down," Chantraine reported. "Almost at once, far from the nausea I had expected, an invigorating warmth, almost like that which follows a drink of raw alcohol, pervaded my body, spreading through my limbs at an incredible speed.

"The union had been sanctified. . . .

"I smeared my fingers over my eyelids and cheeks, as I had seen him do. And for the first time in my life, I felt that I really belonged out there in the kingdom of ice."

And so here was another side to the sealers' philosophy, the dark side. We had heard the economic argument, that any interference on our part would be meddling with the very livelihood of the Newfound-landers, and we had watched members of Parliament in Ottawa leap to amend the Seal Protection Act whenever we hinted at some course of action—Were we going to use helicopters? Why, then, they'd quickly add a clause to the Act that makes it a criminal offense to fly low over seals. Were we threatening to land our helicopters near the herd? Quick, somebody amend the law to make that illegal, too! Were we suggesting we might spray green or red dye on the white pelts of harp seal pups to make their fur commercially worthless? Hurry up and write a ban specifically against that! And on top of all this we even caught a broadside of mind-your-own-business jin-goism from a Newfoundland broadcaster-writer named Rex Murphy, who called Greenpeacers "noxious twits" and said we should all stay home for the winter with "coloring books and paint-by-number sets . . . and the latest Joan Baez songbook." And now we know there is that darker aspect, too, the savage side of human nature, the almost cannibalistic urge to kill and then ingest one's victims.

Nothing the Canadian government in Ottawa could do would dissuade us from going after the sealers in helicopters. The distances, the barrenness of the ter-rain, and, above all, the hostility of both the people and the geography—these factors alone dictated the neces-sity of traveling by helicopter. Our plan was to fly out on the Labrador Front, locate the sealing fleet and the herd from the air, swoop down as close as possible, land, and go into action. The dye we would use to spray the baby seals would be totally harmless to them. However, it would be indelible, or virtually so. Our idea was to mark up the snow-white pelts enough to make them lose their enormous market value *in toto*. By the time our dye faded or grew out, the seals' coats would have darkened, for baby harp seals are "whitecoats" only for the first six weeks of their lives. After that, they would have no special value.

We had it in mind to use either green dye, as green was pretty well established as the Greenpeace color and recognized around the world as the color for all conservationist causes, or red dye, to symbolize the blood of the slaughtered seals. There was some thought of flying very low and spraying as we hovered, but it seemed unlikely, even from the start, that we could work out all the tactics and techniques such an intricate set of maneuvers might involve. Early on, we settled on the plan to fly in by helicopter, get as close as possible, and go the rest of the way across the ice on foot.

We had expected heavy opposition from the Canadian government officials most intimately involved, as well as from some members of Parliament. But we were a little surprised that we also seemed to have stirred up resistance in the Canadian news media. Still, we were getting attention. And that was all to the good. We knew that we had a very powerful magnet for our cause in baby harp seals as an issue. Nobody could fail to be moved at the thought of such beautiful, innocent creatures being killed and skinned. If we could stir up a controversy about baby harp seals, we knew we could hope to influence public opinion in favor of our actions on behalf of all sea mammals. The more cries of outrage we provoked from pro-sealers, the more we knew we were on the right track.

With our eye on the mid-March beginning of the 1976 harp seal hunt in Newfoundland, we opened our publicity campaign in November of 1975. We never let up. Not a week passed, even during the Christmas holidays and the start of the new year, that we did not put out some sort of a public statement or news story. For example, a detailed account of our plans to fight for the seals, with a picture of Bob Hunter and me standing in front of an "Arctic survival dome," published in the Vancouver *Sun,* attracted wide public attention to our campaign.

The survival domes were excellent for our purpose. Manufactured in Vancouver, they were spheres of fiberglass and polyurethane, and consequently very light and easily transported. They came in six sections, and, when put together on the ice and insulated with foam, they would keep the bitter cold from us as we bedded down during the several days we would be confronting the Canadian and Norwegian seal hunters. In the photograph, we plastered the dome with a United Nations flag and Greenpeace posters. And Mike McRae, president of SPACE International, which made and sold the ten-foot-diameter, pumpkinlike shelters for $3,500 each, announced he would help raise money for the seal expedition, *Greenpeace VI,* by raffling off one dome to the public. We expected the expedition to cost $130,000; it ultimately cost that and more.

"Once the sealers arrive," I told a press conference in my role as expedition leader, "we'll move our spraying operations to the area of the hunt, running in front and spraying the seals. If need be, we'll pick up the seals and run away with them. If we can't make it in time, we will shield the seals from the hunters' clubs with our bodies."

We also had thought that we might claim the seals we could rescue as property of the United Nations. But, as with other projected courses of action, some members of Parliament won amendments to the Seal Protection Act to make any such attempt a violation of that law.

We were getting all sorts of threats from the sealers in Gander, Newfoundland—warnings that anybody who tried to interfere with the seal hunt would be summarily shot, and things like that. And from Ottawa, some official, usually Minister of Fisheries Romeo LeBlanc, would promise us jail if we showed up at the hunt. The Newfoundlanders are normally a warm and friendly people. But they grumbled that, if we appeared, *we* would wind up painted red or green.

We received strong support from Brigitte Bardot. The French film star, who is enormously popular among ethnically French Canadians, announced in Paris that she would join us in protesting the 1976 hunt. She put together a camera crew and started for the Gulf of St. Lawrence with plans to make a documentary motion picture about the confrontation. At London's Heathrow Airport, however, she became too ill to continue her journey and returned to Paris in tears. By the time she recovered her health, the 1976 hunt was over, but she led protests in early April outside the Norwegian embassy in Paris, joining her demonstrators in chanting, "Norwegians, murderers!" and "Arrest the seal-killers!" The embassy allowed her inside, and she made her protest to officials there on behalf of herself, the French Animal Protection Society, and her own wildlife-protection organization.

It was March 2, 1976, when we headed for the Labrador Front. As leader, I chose my close friend and comrade at Wounded Knee, David Garrick, as my deputy. To Bob Hunter, then president of the Greenpeace Foundation, it was "the craziest campaign yet," but he was bubbling over with enthusiasm when we left by train from Vancouver. Ten of us were together on the cross-country trip: Hunter, Garrick, and I, plus Michael Chechik, Eileen Chivers, Marilyn Kaga, Bonnie MacLeod, Pat Moore, Henrietta Nielsen, and Ron Precious. We picked up six more expedition members—Al Johnson, Rod Marining, Paul Morse, Paul Spong, Marvin Storrow, and Dan Willens.

The propaganda battle continued as our train carried us from the Pacific to the Atlantic coasts of Canada. To counter our announced plans for flying over the seals in helicopters and spraying them in that fashion, the Canadian government had written into the Seal Protection Act provisions to prohibit aircraft from flying lower than two thousand feet over the seal herds or landing within a half-mile of them. We fired off protests that this was an unenforceable law because the area in question was outside the twelve-mile limit to which Canadian suzerainty extended. Canadian Fisheries Minister LeBlanc fired back that, be that as it may, he would have officials on hand to enforce the law and make arrests. One government official biologist told news reporters that any use of dye on the seal pups would cause them to be rejected by their mothers. But other reputable scientists joined us in collapsing that myth, asking at the same time whether a pup denied mother's milk was worse off than one with his head bashed in and his fur yanked off of him. We all enjoyed this propaganda tomfoolery, and we thought we were getting the better of the give and take. Nevertheless, we were dead serious about our undertaking, and those of us who had been on the ice before were not approaching the experience lightly. We knew that the floes could break up without warning and float away and that sudden storms could also pose serious dangers for our helicopter operations.

We all piled out of the train in North Sydney, Nova

Scotia, at one o'clock in the morning on March 9, 1976. There was a bad storm brewing, as we were warned repeatedly, but we wanted to get on with our trek, so we rented a van and made our way to the ferry that runs to Port-aux-Basques on the southern tip of Newfoundland. The ferry ride is an overnight journey, and we banged and crashed as we pushed through the worst blizzard most of us had ever seen. Great ice floes, known as "pans" in the area, vied with giant ridges of ice in blocking the slow progress of the ferry. We felt our way through the "slop," the local name for the mixture of water and chopped-up ice, and just as dawn was breaking, we reached Newfoundland itself. Port-aux-Basques was little more than a collection of wooden shacks set among ice-coated rocks.

We rented another van, so that we would have more room for ourselves and all the equipment, and set out for St. Anthony. The wind began to rise and soon we had what seemed like a full-force blizzard going as we groped in our two vehicles along the narrowing road leading to our destination. It was miserably cold, and, with visibility obscured to virtually zero, we kept running off the highway and plowing into great snowdrifts.

We stopped at a small motel, to get warm and to get something to eat and drink. Despite hard looks from people at the bar and pool tables, we decided to spend the night. On television, we saw news footage of demonstrations going on in St. Anthony—men waving signs and shouting in thirty-below weather, waiting for us at the town's only entrance. They looked mean, with scars on their faces and icicles in their beards.

Early the next morning, with the storm over and the skies clear, we continued our journey. We had no idea what awaited us, but the view along the way was so spec-

tacular that it was hard to dwell for very long on our
uncertain future. We drove all morning with the hazy
jumble of icebergs and floes in the Gulf of St. Lawrence
on our left and the equally frozen wasteland of Newfoundland on our right. On the radio news broadcasts
we heard that our reception committee had assembled
in St. Anthony once more.

Pat Moore was driving the lead van and I was in the
front seat beside him. Close behind me was Bob Hunter.
We had agreed that the three of us would get out and
confront the Newfoundlanders waiting for us, and
everybody else in our party would stay in the two vans.
The second van was being driven by Al Johnson, a very
dependable man and a skillful driver, by occupation a
jet airline pilot.

After a long stretch of straight road, we went around
a curve and there they were. There must have been two
hundred of them, all in parkas that were predominately
black in color. They were waving signs that said,
"Greenpeace Out!" and "Mainlanders Go Home!" Some
were holding ropes with nooses on them, swinging them
ominously. About forty vehicles were parked crazily
about the road—cars, trucks, and snowmobiles—and
there was nothing for us to do but stop.

"We seem to be here," Moore said. He turned off
the ignition key, sighed, and opened the door on his
side. He got out. I did the same on my side, with Bob
Hunter at my heels.

The Newfoundlanders swarmed around us. Their
signs banged against us and against the van. They seized
the van and began rocking it. Men with enraged faces
bellied up to me and screamed in my face. I could not
pick out the words, but it was clear they were sputtering
out hatred, not arguing but only mouthing slogans. I

caught sight of Pat Moore. He was getting the same
treatment. Like me, he was dressed in a bright orange
survival suit, and both of us could have been picked out
from a mile away in that angry sea of black. In the confusion, I lost sight of Bob Hunter. He was wearing a
navy blue jacket and blended right in with our noisy
greeters.

Pat Moore and I held our ground as best we could
amid all the jostling. When we were able, we engaged
the men in arguments. With a great effort, I forced
myself to grow calmer and calmer as the men grew
angrier. But things were in danger of getting out of
hand all the same. Just then, Eileen Chivers stepped out
of her van and tossed her dark hair loosely over her
shoulders. The sight of a woman dressed like us in
bright orange had an immediate calming effect on that
black-tempered crowd of outdoorsmen. They quieted
noticeably and eased off enough to give us more breath-
ing room. The shouting match went on, with Eileen
joining Pat and me, but her presence had obviously
taken the steam out of the confrontation.

A man on the perimeter—I later learned he was Roy
Pilgrim, who had created and was running an organization called the Concerned Citizens Committee of St.
Anthony Against Greenpeace—started yelling louder
than all the others until things truly quieted down. He
then announced that we would break off our session
and reassemble, as previously arranged, at nine o'clock
that night at the St. Anthony Elementary School auditorium.

"Makes no difference," one man shouted. "These
b'ys are gonna be on their way back to the mainland by
midnight!"

Everybody cheered and there was a general rush for

the cars, trucks, and snowmobiles. We were convoyed into town, some vehicles in front of us and some in back, amid a great deal of shouts and horn-blowing. We were led to the door of Decker's Boardinghouse, where we had made reservations months earlier. It was a pleasant enough two-story house overlooking a frozen bay.

When we telephoned our office in Vancouver, we learned that the Canadian government, by an order-in-council (which requires no Parliamentary action), had outlawed any spraying of seals, such as we intended. The penalty was one thousand dollars fine or one year in prison.

It fell to Bob Hunter, as president of Greenpeace, to make the decision as to strategy and tactics. Bob reviewed the situation: Fisheries Minister LeBlanc had sworn to use every means at his disposal to stop us from interfering with the seal hunt. The latest means handed him by Ottawa would make it possible for him and his cohorts to lock us all up if we tried to put dye on the pups, and the hunt would go on while we languished in jail, totally ineffective. The Newfoundlanders who had become so worked up over our presence were concerned primarily about interference with individual hunting, not the organized activities by Canadian and Norwegian sealing ships out on the Labrador Front; if some sort of bargain were not struck with the Newfoundlanders in St. Anthony, we might never be allowed to proceed out to the ice.

I was against compromising. I wanted to go ahead as we had planned, to escape from this wrought-up crowd somehow, save as many pups as possible, and take the consequences. But the decision was to be otherwise.

That night, about six hundred townspeople were gathered at the school auditorium. It seemed that the whole town had turned out for what had become one of the biggest events in the community's history. It was also a media event, with reporters on hand from Canada and Germany as well as a camera crew from France. We received telephone calls from the United States—from the Washington *Post* and the National Broadcasting Company.

Pat Moore and I spoke first for our viewpoint, after Roy Pilgrim had worked up the crowd with a speech about how sensible and courageous Newfoundlanders are and how they would never allow the likes of us to come from the other side of the continent to tell them what to do. Then Pat and I pushed ahead with our environmental arguments. We were booed and heckled. But when Bob Hunter ended his litany of Greenpeace accomplishments with the surprise announcement that we were abandoning plans to spray the pups, the jeers turned to cheers. It was firm confirmation that the townspeople's hostility was directed toward interference with their traditional practice of sorting out to the herd on their own. They were not concerned about the sealing ships.

Our supporters in Vancouver, however, expressed disappointment and dismay. Some of them even crushed their Greenpeace buttons and mailed them in a brown paper bag to Hunter. Charges of "sell-out" were to haunt us for years afterward.

The helicopters we had chartered arrived from Sept-Iles, Quebec, just before dark on our second day at St. Anthony. Flying them were two very able pilots, Jack Wallace and Birnd Firnung, and we began immediately to use our sleek Bell Jetrangers, with their neoprene-rubber landing floats, to transport fuel, tents, and supplies to our forward base at Belle Isle, some thirty miles to the north.

Before moving some of our crew out to the frozen forward base that Friday, March 12, we had a meeting with leaders of the Newfoundland Fishermen, Food and Allied Workers Union. We had been talking to these labor people about some kind of joint action that might have an impact on the government in Ottawa. At our meeting, we worked out a joint statement that called on Canada to establish a two-hundred-mile fishing management zone in the area. The idea was to keep out foreign fishermen like the Norwegians. In Ottawa, this unity between the Greenpeace Foundation and a labor organization with nine thousand members was unsettling to the government. But we knew, like everybody else involved, that there was virtually no chance that the proposal would ever be acted upon.

Setting up our forward base seemed like landing on a moon that was thirty-five degrees below zero. Nine of us camped at Belle Isle, which is so remote and valueless that people of the area are not sure whether it is northernmost Newfoundland or southeasternmost Labrador. The nine at Belle Isle were Hunter and I, plus Chivers, Garrick, Johnson, Kaga, Moore, Precious, and Storrow. A French photographer named Jean-Claude Francolon came along, too. But only four of us stayed—Garrick, Johnson, Moore, and I—for the two days of a storm that reduced the world around us to a howling, blinding nightmare. We bundled up with every piece of potentially warming material we could find, and we moved like zombies, when we moved at all, spending most of our time simply lying in our thin little tents, waiting for the ordeal to end.

Our camp was atop cliffs that towered eight

hundred feet above the jagged ice that surrounded it in a jumble of pans that crunched and creaked as they whirled in tidal streams or rafted upon each other at pressure points, splitting open at times to expose "leads" of open water. Before the winds came howling, we could hear the movement of the ice from many miles around. Beneath the cliffs, vaulted caverns threaded their way inland for a hundred feet and more. The island was uninhabited, covered entirely with a sheet of crystal-hard ice, its only structure a little lighthouse, abandoned now but occupied by a keeper in summer.

When it seemed we could no longer endure the storm, it ended. The hurricane-force winds had driven us to move the camp to a less-exposed site, and we had burrowed into sleeping bags inside our tents like hibernating bears for the worst of the blow. Now we awoke to an eerie stillness. The pop and crack of the restless ice on the Labrador Front sounded like gunfire. It was Friday, March 19— the day the 1976 harp seal hunt officially began.

The morning was brilliant. Its peace was shattered, though, by the clatter of what seemed to our sleepy eyes to be a sky full of helicopters. They whirled above our cliffs: two Fisheries Ministry helicopters; one Bell Jetranger like our two, with Brian Davies at the controls, and another half-dozen or so bearing reporters and television crews, as well as a Brian Davies inspiration—a group of airline stewardesses he had brought in as guests of his International Fund for Animal Welfare. Rick Cashin, president of the fishermen's union, had denounced Davies as exploiting both the hunt and the stewardesses to advance the cause of his animal welfare organization, but nobody could deny that Brian knew how to put the horror of the hunt on prime-time television with full photogenic impact.

It was 6:45 A.M.—the first morning of the hunt—when our helicopters arrived at Belle Isle to take us out on the ice floe. Aboard with our pilots, Jack Wallace and Birnd Firnung, were the others of our forward ice party, plus Art Elliott, the local guide who could lead us across the treacherous pans and leads. It is hard to describe how good it felt to be moving again, after having been pinned down by the storm, and there was a tingly sense of exhilaration and anticipation flowing through all of us as we settled in for the search for the sealing ships and the herd.

We had a pretty good idea of where they were, or, rather, where they were supposed to be. The storm had scrambled everything. Instead of pressing on, the ships had simply stopped dead. As a result, our calculations were off, and our first helicopter sortie was fruitless. We saw nothing but icy desolation in all directions and we were forced to return to Belle Isle for refueling. Our first rush of adrenalin was wasted. We set out across the ice in our brightly painted choppers a second time, and that was the charm.

Our estimations were more exact the second time out, for, after about twenty minutes at about three thousand feet, we spotted a couple of black specks on the horizon. Soon we were over them and saw they were the *Martin Karlsen* and the *Theron,* sealing ships registered in Canada but Norwegian-owned. They were a couple of hundred yards apart, doing about five knots as they churned through the "slop" ice that was a mixture of ice and water and offered little resistance.

The Canadian sealing ship *Arctic Explorer,* out of Halifax, was at another location, we learned later, and at that very moment was being bedeviled by Brian Davies, his stewardesses, and a coterie of television cameramen, photographers, and reporters.

We dropped low over the two ships we had found, exhilarated by our success in tracking them down despite their radio silence and other ruses to avoid detection. We were so low that we could see the little yellow buttons worn by the unsmiling men on deck—the badge that announced they had paid their dollar for a license as "swilers," which is what Newfoundlanders call those who kill seals. We checked the path of these vessels, wheeled and climbed, and turned in the same direction of their heading.

The ice began to look more coalesced and seemed to grow thicker. We realized that this was the Labrador Front itself, solid enough and stable enough to provide mother seals with a place to bear their young and to protect them until they were strong enough to fend for themselves. It was a place, too, where the swilers would soon find them both, trusting and vulnerable.

We saw more black specks and counted them. Eight. This would be the main body. And this would be the herd.

Closer, we saw something else. The ruggedly configured ice looked as if it had served as a battleground. Great smears of blood stained long, crimson streaks in the diamond-hard ice, and there were patches where more blood had been let than in other places. And there were, too, incongruous patches in the trail—caused, it soon became apparent, when an ice pan broke loose and flipped over to present its pristine underside.

"Well, boys," Jack said, bringing the helicopter to a rest on the ice as close to the herd as he dared. "We've got them for you. It's up to you now."

The baby seals were all around us, beautiful beyond expectation. Chubby little bundles of soft white fur, their round, jet-black eyes glistening with tears, they cried, sounding exactly like human infants in distress.

Intermittently, this cooing signal rose to a shriek coun-
terpointed by the whack and thud of the Norwegians'
hak-a-piks.

Out of the helicopter, I began to trot over the slip-
pery, shifting ice toward the bulk of the herd, a couple
of miles away. I became aware suddenly that we were
quite distinguishable, like opposing teams: sealers in
grays and blacks, methodically chopping and skinning,
and Greenpeacers in orange survival suits and hoods,
bright as a flame against the total whiteness and rushing
forward with outstretched hands.

I was aware that Art Elliott, our Newfoundlander
guide, and David Garrick were running along with me.
The others fanned out nearby. As we came in among
the Norwegians, I saw Al Johnson stop between a burly
sealer and a pup and throw himself on top of the seal.
The sealer turned away and headed for another victim.
But David beat him to it and covered that pup with his
body. The sealer hesitated and then started walking
toward the nearest ship, the *Melshorn.*

Pat Moore had a camera, and he snapped a mother
seal rocking back and forth over what was left of her
pup—the raw-red carcass that sealers call a "sculp" once
they have stripped off its coat. The pup's eyes were
open and staring but lustreless.

I threw myself between a sealer and his prey, and,
when he shrugged and walked off, I followed him and
did it again. I blocked another sealer nearby. I could see
other orange-clad figures doing the same, and, to my
surprise, I could hear myself swearing in Norwegian—
part of my education as a deckboy in the Pacific and
Indian Oceans in 1969 and 1970 aboard the Norwegian
motorship *Bris.* The Norwegian sealers seemed taken
aback.

It was maddening to see how little effect we were

having on the hunt. There were so few of us and so many of them. We simply could not be in enough places at the right time to save enough seals. The Norwegians were swearing, and I was swearing, and I became aware also that two men were chasing after me, shouting for me to stop interfering and announcing that they were inspectors with the Canadian Ministry of Fisheries.

By that time, I had worked to within a few yards of the *Melshorn*. It was methodically moving into the melee, crashing forward in the ice for a dozen or so feet, halting and backing off, and then plunging ahead once more. Each time it rammed, it crunched a fresh path, and whatever was in the way was mangled amid the great boulders of ice churned up by the weighted bow. Harp seals that happened to be on its course, mothers and pups, had left a trail of blood on either side of the *Melshorn*.

As the ship cranked up for another charge, I saw a baby seal sitting placidly about eight feet from the edge of the ice. I vowed the ship would not have it. I raced over, and, as the *Melshorn* bore down, I scooped up the pup in my arms—nearly falling over under the weight of it, about sixty pounds—and stumbled and fell out of danger. The pup first bit me on the cheek, and then it wiggled in my arms, as if nestling in for a more comfortable fit. I looked down into its ebony eyes, which looked back quizzically with such innocence that I burst into tears.

Well away from the hunt, I found an isolated area and freed the pup. I did not look back as it waddled away. Now, I was personally involved, not simply making a protest of principle. I had saved that particular pup's life, held it in my arms, felt its warm body against mine.

Exhausted, we boarded our helicopters for the trip back to Belle Isle. We had to get off the ice before dusk, for it was far too dangerous to be out there at night. For better or worse, we had done our best. The three Canadian and five Norwegian vessels reported taking 13,600 pelts on that first day. They kept no record on the total body count.

For the next three days, one of the worst blizzards in history for the area struck our base camp. Winds gusted up to 100 miles per hour, and it was all we could do to keep our tents from blowing over the cliffs. The only good thing about the weather was that it held up the seal hunt for three days as well. At the first break, when our helicopters could fly, we evacuated Belle Isle for St. Anthony. When we returned a few days later, everything had been swept away by the storm.

Once more, we flew out across the floes, guessing the whereabouts of the hunt again, as the Canadian officials on hand continued to withhold information from us. Once more, we were lucky. About eighty miles offshore, we spotted a group of Canadian sealers. We landed and went over to them. The men were surly and threatening. They stopped killing pups when they saw our camera. We tried talking to them. I sought to engage one man in a discussion about why we believed the killing should stop, but he would not respond. All the while, he held a skinning knife, dripping with blood, about three inches from my abdomen. His face and hands were encrusted with the rusty redness of dried blood. When we left, I knew they would resume the killing.

On the way back to our helicopters, Bob Hunter and I expressed to each other our sense of frustration at this encounter. We both wondered what we could do there. How could we demonstrate to these men, and to our cameras, how determined we were to save seals? The idea came to us as we watched the *Arctic Endeavour* plowing its scarlet-stained hull through the ice. What if we could stop the ship? If the ship could not proceed, the hunt could not proceed.

About twenty feet in front of the ship we found a baby seal. We planted ourselves protectively over it and stood side by side, our backs turned to the *Arctic Endeavour*. We could feel and hear the ship as it plunged forward and pulled back. The ice under our feet vibrated. The ship's diesel engines clanked and rattled with each effort.

A crewman at the starboard side of the bow who had been attaching a winch line to a bundle of blood-soaked pelts yelled down to us from his perch about three stories above our heads. His accent was pure Newfoundland:

"Y'betta move, b'ys. The ol' man ain't one t'tink twice about runnin ya into the ice!"

Bob Hunter yelled back:

"Tell the old bastard to do what he wants! We're not moving!"

The ship stopped and backed off, and for a moment Bob and I thought we had won. But then the *Arctic Endeavour* came at us again, and this time it seemed to be moving with even more speed. We could feel her coming and hear her, and it took an act of will not to turn around to see where she was. The ice trembled and cracked when she hit and kept on coming. The heavy vibrations of the engines tingled in the soles of our feet. Great blocks of ice tumbled before the bow and nudged our boots.

The crewman in the bow screamed:

"Stop 'er, Cap! Stop 'er! The stupid asses ain't movin'!"

The *Arctic Endeavour* came to a dead stop, backed up, and halted five feet behind our backs. I picked up the baby seal and started walking, trying to be as casual and calm as possible and looking for a place of safety for it.

A man in a Fisheries Ministry uniform blocked my way. He had a camera and he took my picture. He pulled some papers from his pocket and began reading from the various new "Greenpeace" amendments to the Seal Protection Act:

"Section 21 (B) states that it is a federal offense to remove a seal from one location to another. It is an offense to pick up a live seal from the ice. You are in violation of this regulation."

I could feel the anger rising, flushing my cheeks.

"Do you mean to tell me," I asked, "that I'm supposed to leave this baby to be crushed by that ship?"

"That's no business of yours," he replied. "The law is the law. I don't make the laws, I just enforce them."

I snorted and brushed past, tightening my grip on the baby seal. I could not believe that the Canadian government would try to enforce its laws in international waters. And I hated being put on the spot like that by Ottawa. Clearly, I could not allow the pup to die. It was up to the Fisheries Ministry man now to make his move, and he apparently decided to do nothing. He simply watched in silence as I went as far away as seemed safe and released the baby seal. The pup looked at me quizzically for a few seconds, turned, and flip-flopped away until its whiteness blended in with the whiteness of the ice and it was gone.

Back at the *Arctic Endeavour,* Bob Hunter was still blocking the ship's path. I returned and stood with him. We did not know how long we could continue our picketing, for night was fast approaching. Our pilots were agitating for prompt departure, and we acceded. Jack Wallace was particularly concerned, for his aircraft was low on fuel and we expected headwinds on the way back to St. Anthony. We made it with seven gallons to spare.

"I've never cut it that close," Jack said.

We had our last contact with the sealing fleet of 1976 on Saturday, March 20. We were aloft in our helicopters by eight o'clock on what seemed to be the coldest day of all. Veterans of the Labrador Front by now, our pilots headed straight for the fleet. Once there, however, they made certain that they did not violate the two-thousand-foot ceiling of the amended Seal Protection Act, or come down anywhere near a seal. After about twenty minutes of hovering and circling, they picked out a spot and went in.

Immediately, two Fisheries Ministry helicopters came pounding in. Officers told Jack Wallace and Bernd Firnung that they had violated the law by landing less than one-half nautical mile from a seal on the ice and by flying below two thousand feet over the seals. Wallace and Firnung were arguing heatedly with the government representatives as I walked away in the direction of the seals. The last I heard as I moved out of earshot was the pilots' demanding to see the seal involved and the official saying it had dived into the water.

We set off across the ice towards the operating ship, which happened to be the *Arctic Explorer*. The scene was by far the goriest and most nauseating we had ever seen. Great gobs of blood had coagulated in puddles on the ice and, in places, had even pitted the ice with its heat before cooling off. Hundreds upon hundreds of skinned bodies lay piled all around, glazed eyes staring out accusingly. Occasionally, we met a whimpering survivor, ducking its head behind a snowbank.

Suddenly, before we could go into action among the working sealers, both of our helicopters came roaring up. They landed and our crew members inside beckoned us toward them. Everybody, including the pilots, seemed to be yelling at once.

"Whiteout!" they shouted. "Whiteout coming! Hurry! Let's get out of here!"

The Fisheries Ministry people had allowed the helicopters to pursue us, and now it was a race against the sudden blinding storm. At full throttle, as the blizzard arrived and grew in intensity, we beat our way back to St. Anthony, skimming precariously close to the ice as the pilots fought for shelter from the wind wherever they could find protuberances. It seemed to take forever to reach home.

Before the day was out, however, the Royal Canadian Mounties called on our pilots and charged them formally with breaking the Seal Protection Act. They were not jailed but the helicopters were confiscated. Two Mounties stood guard around the clock at a rope fence surrounding the machines. Bond for them was set at twenty thousand dollars, and it took us almost a week to raise the money and take off for another run at the fleet. By that time, the Labrador Front had floated out of our range, and we knew our mission was all over, for better or worse.

We returned to Ottawa, knowing we had not saved the lives of many baby seals, but knowing, too, that we had kicked up a hell of a row over the annual massacre. We had planted some seeds of doubt in the minds of quite a few people in Canada and around the world, and, perhaps best of all, exercised our protest muscles in a worthy cause and picked up more pointers on how to do a better job next time.

And there would certainly be a next time.

6

Whale War Two

IN THE SPRING OF 1976, we turned our attention to *Greenpeace VII*—our second expedition to save the whales. We called it, among ourselves, "Whale War Two."

We were growing expert in the propaganda arts and were fully aware that, no matter how boldly (foolishly, some said) we risked our lives, our efforts would all be wasted unless we could focus public attention on the message: Quit killing sea mammals. Because our organization was gaining credibility there was a growing recognition of the validity of our cause. We were being asked, for example, to lecture at universities and before civic and service clubs, and we sent a delegate (myself) to the Marine Mammal Conference in Bergen, Norway. The word was out.

Yet, as a technical matter, we wanted to improve our confrontation capabilities. This time, as we prepared for another run at the whalers in the Pacific—the Japanese as well as the Soviets—we vowed never again to put to sea in a boat that was too slow. Our faithful old *Phyllis Cormack* was no match for the Soviet killer ships. Her genteel eight knots was frustratingly ineffective against the harpooners' twenty knots.

And so this time we sought a faster, more maneuverable vessel. George Korotva found her in Seattle, Washington. She was the *James Bay,* wood-hulled and 150 feet long, built in 1956 as a minesweeper for the Canadian Navy. Her speed could outclass the Soviets', and she was available at a reasonable price. She was a sister ship of the *Edgewater Fortune,* which we had sailed in our 1971 protest against the Amchitka tests, so we could judge her performance possibilities on the basis of that experience.

This time, we planned to have six or seven *kamikaze* inflatable boats aboard, more sophisticated navigational equipment, and a larger crew—nearly three dozen, compared with the thirteen aboard the eighty-seven-foot *Phyllis Cormack.* We set to work immediately, furiously converting the *James Bay* to our specifications, using volunteer labor wherever possible. She was far from ready, but, as before, we had committed ourselves to a sailing date. On June 14, amid great fanfare (including a rock-and-country concert that raised nearly thirty thousand dollars for expenses), we sailed away from Vancouver's Jericho Bay docks.

The *James Bay* was a beauty. Her sparkling white hull, lovingly painted and decorated by our volunteers, bore her name proudly at the bow, with a great rainbow punctuated by three bright stars, and, from amidships aft, a line drawing of a sperm whale and her baby bearing, in English and Japanese, the legend:

SAVE THE WHALES — SAVE THE EARTH

We made a grand exit from the wood docks, crowded once again with well-wishers and festooned with blue United Nations banners and the flags of many countries. But we went only as far as Sydney, on the southern tip of Vancouver Island, where for the next five days—until our actual sailing on June 19—we worked on the engines, tested electronic gear, and completed a host of final chores like taking on water and blowing up the inflatable boats.

Alongside us at the dock in Sydney was the *Phyllis Cormack,* all scrubbed up and with her own rainbow at the hull, plus her own slogan:

SAVE GOD'S WHALES

Captain John Cormack was again at the helm. Despite pressure from the Vancouver fishery, which wanted him to seine for halibut, he had elected to lease his boat to a California group that called itself the Mendocino Whale War Committee. It conducted its operations independently of ours. We met briefly at San Francisco, but this group did not come out with us into the Pacific, choosing instead to patrol along the California coastline as a kind of backup to our searchings farther out to sea.

Our thirty-two-member crew at the outset included Bob Hunter as overall leader, George Korotva as captain, and myself as first mate. The others comprised a mixed bag of veterans and newcomers: Bob Hunter's wife, Bobbi, plus Chris Aikenhead, Mike Bailey, Eileen Chivers, Lance Cowan, Bruce Drummond, Fred Easton, David Garrick, Melville Gregory, Ted Haggerty, Matt Herron, Al Hewitt, Marilyn Kaga, Bruce Kerr, Mary Lee, Susi Leger, Michael Manolson, Rod Marining, Taeko Miwa, Pat Moore, Ron Precious, Paul Spong, Kazumi Tanaka, Bob Thomas, Alan Wade, Don Webb, Rex Weyler, David Wise, and Gary Zimmerman. As we pressed our hunt for the whalers, the lineup changed somewhat. Some people left and others came on, for various reasons, but this was how we started out.

Sailing south, we tested our radio directional equipment and other gear, more or less shaking down the ship and crew. We put in at Portland, Oregon, to take on water and touch base with supporters of our effort and arrived in San Francisco, California, on July 1—expecting to make final preparations there. What we found, however, was a city making its own gigantic preparations to celebrate the two-hundredth anniversary of the independence of the United States: July 4, 1976.

The entire city of San Francisco was having a party. We participated by taking some of the local Greenpeacers for a ride in San Francisco Bay aboard the Zodiac inflatables. Everybody got thoroughly wet as we zipped around the harbor, circling Alcatraz Island, the "Rock" that is now deserted but once was the site of a federal prison, and going as close as the U.S. Coast Guard would allow to the aircraft carrier *Coral Sea,* the biggest among some five hundred vessels that made up the Bicentennial Celebration flotilla. Among them was the fireboat *Alert,* delightfully spraying red, white, and blue water all day long. That night, thousands of people crowded the docks for a fireworks demonstration launched from Alcatraz. Unhappily, the fog that San Francisco is so famous for rolled in so densely that we could see only dim flashes in the mist.

While Bob Hunter and some of the others met with conservation groups in the area to further our on-going effort to raise funds for fuel and supplies, we busied ourselves aboard ship. Marilyn Kaga and Susi Leger painted the foredeck and sprinkled fine sand on it to provide an abrasive footing; when the deck was dry, Lance Cowan and I washed it down to get rid of excess sand. To correct a tendency we had noted in the *James Bay* to pitch and roll too much, we took on about twenty tons of sand for ballast. It was back-breaking work to fill up hundreds of sacks with eighty pounds of sand in each and hoist them aboard for stacking in the port and starboard midships lockers, along with a few at the stern and forward.

Finally, after one last effort to raise funds by hawking Greenpeace T-shirts and other souvenir items, we cleared port for our searching run to Honolulu. At nightfall on July 12, we passed the Golden Gate Bridge, outward bound.

At this point, our crew had changed slightly. Bruce Drummond, Taeko Miwa, and Don Webb had left the ship at San Francisco, where we took on two newcomers—Dr. Norman Seaton, representing Cleveland Amory and the Fund for Animals, which had made a sizeable donation, and Barry Lavender, a fellow Vancouverite.

Cleveland Amory, the driving force behind the Fund for Animals, which has emerged as one of the world's most energetic and successful conservation groups, was extremely supportive of our efforts then, and, throughout the years, he has never wavered. In 1976, when we set out after the Pacific whalers, I had not yet met Amory. That good fortune did not come until 1977, when we both attended a wildlife symposium conducted in St. Louis, Missouri. But I certainly knew about him and his work on behalf of animals, and I had read his book, *Mankind? Our Incredible War on Wildlife,* published in 1974. And I knew, too, that he was a celebrated author and columnist, a proper Bostonian out of Milton Academy and Harvard, who had, indeed, written a book called *The Proper Bostonians,* published in 1947, as well as other best-sellers.

In the world of animal-loving activists, Cleveland Amory is a revered figure. A giant in body as well as spirit (he is six feet, four inches tall and well over two hundred and fifty pounds, and his executive assistant, Marian Probst, calls him "The Bear"), Amory has made possible much of the work that some of the others of us have done. He once told me he decided to create the Fund for Animals, which helps finance the kind of things I organize as protests, after being sickened by a bullfight in Mexico City. He said he was appalled to discover upon checking that no effective anti-bullfighting literature existed—"nothing but Hemingway and others, glorifying this killing as 'sport'!"

Amory is sometimes teased for being disorganized and forgetful, but it has been my observation that he tends to take on more assignments than any one person could handle easily. In 1979, when I went to him for money to stage a double whammy—major protests against both sealing and whaling—he obliged with alacrity. I was grateful for his ability to make quick decisions.

On our 1976 expedition to save the whales, our first three days out of San Francisco were characterized by rough seas and *mal de mer* among the crew. By July 15, both had abated, and we stopped to investigate an unusual drama being played out on the high seas. A half-dozen squawking albatrosses were wheeling over a giant squid, which was about eight feet across and looked to weigh about a hundred and fifty pounds. It appeared to be dying. The birds had pecked out its eyes, but it was still fighting back, although feebly. Gary Zimmerman and I put out a Zodiac and went up for a closer look. I touched a tentacle and the squid squirted a jet of reddish brown ink, its last act before succumbing. Gary and I tried to lift it into the Zodiac, with the albatrosses coming to within two feet of us and denouncing our intrusion in a cacophony of squawks, squeals, and a beating of wings. The squid came apart as it broke water. The birds pounced on its parts, noisily continuing their feeding.

For me, those early days at sea on the 1976 voyage were idyllic and reminded me of a favorite quote: "There are nights at sea of exquisite quiet, the time all mariners love. The sea is smooth and the ship runs proud. The wind is gentle and friendly, and evokes a delicious melancholy, a peace that stirs memories and hopes that lie buried in the bustle of day."

And so it was with me at that time. I found myself, when not on watch or otherwise occupied with ship's business, reading about whales or meditating on them. I had brought along some fairly extensive accounts of whales and whaling, with emphasis on how the animal is inexorably being sacrificed to the industry, and I was struck by this thought: From the Bible's Jonah and his whale to today's $150-million-a-year business, this great "king of the boundless sea" of the sailors' chanty has reigned over fact, fiction, myth, and lore having to do with all things maritime. And the fact, fiction, myth, and lore often become jumbled together so that it is not always easy to tell one from another.

When people talk of whaling, they generally think of Captain Ahab and Moby Dick. They see brave men in small boats boldly confronting a Leviathan the size of thirty elephants. Yet, that has not been the situation since the 1860s, when steam-driven whalers began to replace the schooners, sloops, brigs, and barks. Confronted with such bigger, faster vessels, the whales were no longer free to roam the seas with impunity. Moreover, a sealing captain named Svend Foyn mated the harpoon to a bomb and gave the world of the 1860s its first exploding harpoon. No longer could the immense blue and finback whales swim away, or sound to inaccessible depths with a puny lance in their great backs. The internal explosion usually kills them within minutes—although sometimes a harpooned whale may writhe in agony for hours.

There is nothing glamorous about today's whaling ships, not the mother vessel with its great flensing deck and cookers for the oil, nor the killer ships that hunt down its victims. They stink. They stink so that one is almost certain to retch when first coming upon them. Blackened with the gore of thousands of deaths, chipped and unpainted, dented and unrepaired, they are an insult to the eye. They hiss with pressurized air, roar with the laboring of diesels, clank and groan with the straining of winches, and thus they tear at the ears as well as offend the eye and the nose.

The International Whaling Convention, at first blush, would seem to have taken care of the world's business of protecting the whale. But this agreement, which led at the end of World War II to the creation of the International Whaling Commission, actually has worked to protect the industry. It sought to get the business back to its normal rate of killing after the interruption of the war. The IWC has set quotas and adopted certain regulations—such as prohibiting the killing of nursing calves or mothers, and placing a moratorium on the killing of right whales and Pacific gray whales because of their scarcity. But the commission never has applied effective international controls, and its pious-sounding but toothless regulations simply do not work.

Of the nations that are members of the IWC, Japan and the Soviet Union are the only ones that still maintain extensive whaling fleets. Japan's is by far the larger and farther-ranging, but both countries seem intent on wiping out every species of whale that exists.

Five whaling countries—Chile, the Republic of China, South Korea, Peru, and Spain—only recently joined the IWC. Portugal and Somalia still refuse to do so. Together, these seven accounted for about four thousand whales per year, many of them on the endangered list.

Most of the outlaw ships involved in these operations actually are owned or supported by Japan. The Japanese regularly bought whale meat produced by the pirate whaler *Sierra,* for example, and even kept four Japanese meat merchants aboard at all times to select the best cuts, leaving the rest of the meat and all of the blubber and bones to be thrown into the sea. The selected meat was marked "Produce of Spain" and shipped to Japan via the Ivory Coast. In some cases, it sold for forty dollars per pound.

The *Sierra,* owned by a company registered in Liechtenstein and flying the flag of Somalia, with a Norwegian captain and a South African crew, had been considered in the early 1970s to be secretly owned by Japanese fishing interests. That was when she was accused of nearly destroying the humpback whale population in the Caribbean, despite an IWC ban.

As we sailed the Pacific toward Hawaii in the middle of 1976, these were the facts and figures that outraged me. Such inhumanity toward harmless and beautiful creatures that I knew were endangered made me redouble my determination to keep fighting for their salvation. I reviewed the situation of the great whales, the largest and among the most intelligent animals ever to live on our planet:

• The spectacular blue whale (*Balaenoptera musculus*), the largest creature ever to inhabit the earth. *Guinness*

Book of Records says one female killed in 1947 measured more than ninety feet in length; its tongue weighed 4.7 tons, and its heart fifteen hundred pounds. Yet, its throat is so small that it can swallow no fish larger than a sardine. The U.S. Department of the Interior estimated in 1970 that only six hundred to three thousand remained worldwide.

• The humpback whale (*Megaptera novaeangliae*), whose slightly spooky sounds have been taped and published in a recording (Capitol Records' *Songs of the Humpback Whale,* produced by Dr. Roger S. Payne). The sounds have been identified as proper "songs," in that they are rhythmical, sequential, and repeated, and they last for several minutes. The U.S. Department of Commerce estimates the humpbacks' numbers today at five thousand worldwide, including three thousand in the Southern Hemisphere, where they are openly hunted by Chile and some other nations.

• The bowhead whale (*Balaena mysticetus*), now totaling no more than a few thousand. They are still heavily hunted by Alaskan Eskimos, who traditionally lost four or five they killed for every one they pull out of the water. The rate has improved in recent years.

• The right whale (*Eubalaena glacialis*), nominally protected but so scarce as to be uncountable. The last known colony of southern right whales was sighted in 1962 by a whaling fleet off the South Atlantic islands of Tristan da Cunha. It wiped them out.

• The gray whale (*Eschrichtius robustus*), protected since 1938. They now number a little over ten thousand, migrating along the United States and Mexican coasts in the Pacific. But the Atlantic gray whale (*Eschrichtius gibosus*) has been wiped out in the North Atlantic. It is extinct.

• The sperm whale (*Physeter catadon*), still in sizeable

but very depleted numbers. This whale received protection in July, 1981.

• The fin or finback whale (*Balaenoptera physalus*), like the sperm whale, being rapidly destroyed by the Japanese and Soviets. Second in size only to the blue, it probably is the second largest animal ever to have lived.

• The sei whale (*Balaenoptera borcalis*), like the sperm and the fin, losing way steadily to the onslaught of the Japanese and Soviet whalers.

Craig Van Note, executive vice president of Monitor, a Washington, D.C. consortium of more than thirty conservation groups, has said it all in testimony to the U.S. Congress: "To make margarine, pet and mink food, cosmetics, fertilizer, steaks and lubricating oil, so many whales have been killed that half of the ten species of great whales have been driven to the brink of extinction. The blue, humpback, right and bowhead whales may be doomed, their numbers too few for effective reproduction."

Aboard the *James Bay,* we mulled over such gloomy statistics, assessments, and forecasts during lengthy talk sessions below-decks and while basking in the sun topside. Dr. Paul Spong, who had missed our first confrontation with the Soviets but made sure he came along this time, observed the irony of the situation: "Just as we are beginning to glimpse the incredible nature of whales, we are on the verge of exterminating them."

July 17, 1976, was a Saturday, and the *James Bay* was exactly 980 miles east of Maui in the Hawaiian Islands. Perhaps because it was the weekend, our skipper, George Korotva, stopped the ship about two o'clock in the afternoon and suggested that everybody take a swim. This we did, joyously.

I snorkeled for an hour, inspecting the bottom of the hull in sparkling visibility. Under the water, an inky blue on the surface, one could see for two hundred yards or more. I estimated the depth to be about twelve thousand feet, at almost one thousand miles from the nearest landfall. Plankton was in abundance—flagellates and minute jellyfish—and there was a small crab clinging to the keel. I noticed the port propeller was slightly nicked and I made a mental note to get a hammer and go over the side to fix it the next day. An albatross landed nearby and I swam up under him and tickled his belly. That startled him into considerable splashing around before he took off. He came back, though, as I lay floating on my back, and looked me over intently, as if checking me out as a possible source of food. David Garrick and I later obliged him by throwing him some scraps from the freezer.

That night, as we listened to the radio traffic and worked our radio direction finder, we calculated that the Soviet whaling fleet was close, perhaps less than three hundred miles away, and probably coming toward us. We were worried about fuel. The question was: Should we hook up with the Soviets, interfering with their kills as long as we could before returning to San Francisco to refuel? Should we break off immediately, go back to San Francisco for fuel, and try again? Or should we go on to Maui, refuel, and go off beyond the Hawaiian Islands in search of the Japanese fleet? We had only eight days of fuel. I favored the first option, and, as it turned out, that is the one we followed.

All the next day, July 18, we kept heading toward where we felt the Soviet whalers were operating, keeping our ears glued to the radio and the Russian being spoken over it.

"Yeah, that's the *Dalniy Vostok,* all right," George Korotva said.

Listening, as the only other crew member familiar

with the Russian language, I agreed. It was the same
factory ship we had accosted the year before, the same
whose killer ship had fired a 250-pound, exploding harpoon over our heads as we raced our *kamikaze* Zodiacs
between her bow and the whales. I had an intense feeling of déjà vu. Soon, we would see how much of that old
drama we would repeat.

It was 7:10 on the morning of Monday, July 19,
when our long vigil at the radio paid off. On the horizon, we saw three vessels: one large, two smaller. The
water was smooth as the *James Bay* surged, jumping out
to a closing speed of eighteen knots. My heart was
pounding in my ears, so loud that I could scarcely hear
our boat's engines.

We were 850 miles northeast of Maui, where we
undoubtedly would have to go to refuel soon. We could
afford only a few days with the Russians. We would
have to make them intense, worthwhile days.

Once more I tied a Japanese-like *banzai* scarf around
my head. I aimed my *kamikaze* at one of the Soviet killer
ships marked *PK 2007*. Marilyn Kaga was with me
aboard the Zodiac. She tensed in the bow, squinting
against the wind, as I slammed the throttle all the way
home and our little rubber raft heaved itself half out of
the water.

Bob Hunter, who had been with me in the lead
kamikaze in 1975, was in another Zodiac this time, with
his wife, Bobbi, and Dr. Paul Spong also on board. They
seemed to be having trouble getting their outboard
engine started, and I could hear Bob's voice, high-
pitched and cutting in the calm air, as they all three
pushed and tugged at the recalcitrant machinery. At
long last, they must have done something right, for the
engine sputtered into life. I looked back and I saw two

other Zodiacs milling about near the *James Bay*—one with our movie crew aboard and the other bearing our still-photography people.

After the initial confusion, not at all uncommon in boat launchings, we formed up smartly and raced off full-tilt in the direction of the *PK 2007*.

The killer ship, just as decrepit and unhealthy-looking as the year before, responded almost at once. In the helmsman's spot on the bridge, a man I took to be the captain looked out toward us. I was reminded of the killer-ship skipper who had made the throat-cutting gesture. Was that the way it was to be again? It was eerie, to be back in a Zodiac racing for position between the harpoon and the whales, to play out the same drama again. Or would we? This Soviet skipper had none of the curled-lip arrogance of the other one. I saw no defiance in his face, only his frown. His lips were moving and the veins in his neck stood out. He was apparently barking out orders. Immediately, the squat *PK 2007* settled even more deeply into the water and surged ahead. We raced after her, Marilyn and I in the lead, and I could hear a shout rising up and through my choked-up throat, half-strangling me.

A couple of thousand yards ahead, we saw the killer ship's prey. A pod of sperm whales, five or six of them, had breached with great slaps of their flukes on the choppy waves, and were lolling on the surface.

We sped along with the *PK 2007* like porpoises pacing an ocean liner. We rode her bow wave, and, I noticed, if any of our craft got close to the speeding prow, the captain would speak up and the ship would alter course away from the veering inflatable. The harpooner was at his station in the bow, clenching the handle of the 90-millimeter launcher. The bow bucked and heaved in a great spraying of foam, and the harpooner clung to his bulky weapon, his fingers straying to the trigger occasionally and his head ducking to squint an eye through the pipelike sight.

By now, we had maneuvered our three small boats ahead of the killer ship. We were preparing to get into blocking positions between the harpoon and the whales.

And then I saw the harpooner straighten up and look back down the catwalk to the bridge. He nodded, shook his head, and changed his whole demeanor from alertness to relaxation. He seemed to sag. He shouted something toward the bridge and shook his head again.

Without warning, the *PK 2007* stopped charging. We went spinning off far ahead of her as her bow suddenly settled down from its full-speed-ahead tilt. The killer ship soon was dead in the water.

In our boats, as we wheeled about to come back to her, we all started cheering. There we were—six men and two women in three small craft in the middle of the trackless ocean—screaming our heads off, punching the air with our fists, and jumping up and down as much as we dared without risking a fall overboard.

The Soviet whalers, it seemed, had orders not to endanger us again by firing over our heads. And it seemed clear, too, that their new policy called for an end to whaling while we and our cameras were on the scene.

The *PK 2007* harpooner, looking like a man who had just lost a prize, swirled his cumbersome cannon around and removed the heavy missile from its maw. He racked the harpoon with a dozen others. He covered the launcher with a sheet of green plastic, lashing it securely. *PK 2007* had given up killing whales for the day.

Several hundred yards away, the half-dozen sperm

whales had begun to hyper-ventilate. They were preparing to sound, safe from the harpoon, for the time being at least.

We cut off our engines and sat quietly in our little boats for about twenty minutes, not knowing quite what to do next. The Soviets aboard the killer ship seemed to be equally without a plan. We rocked gently on the choppy sea, listening to the *lap-lap* sounds of the waves against the hull of the *PK 2007*. Soviet seamen stood at the railing of their ship, looking down on us, and we, sitting stiffly, as if we were in church pews, looked up at them. When Marilyn and I talked at all, it was in whispers, and I saw that our colleagues in the other two boats seemed to be doing the same.

The Soviet skipper broke the spell. From the bridge, we could hear him yell, and then the ship's engines coughed into action. We braced for another run under the big bow, but the *PK 2007* merely made a slow, decorous turn and headed at an easy pace back to her mother ship, the *Dalniy Vostok,* off on the far horizon. We trailed along for a short spell and then scooted over to our own mother ship.

Back aboard the *James Bay,* we raced to within five hundred feet of the *Dalniy Vostok* and lay off her starboard aft quarter. The *Dalniy Vostok* was working. Two killer ships flanked her stern and we could hear the clanging of chains and the clashing of gears as dead whales were dragged by winches up the runway of the big vessel's gaping bottom.

We put over a Zodiac, with myself at the throttle and cameramen Matt Herron and Kazumi Tanaka as passengers, and an Avon bearing Pat Moore, Rex Weyler, and Eileen Chivers.

Matt and Kazumi shot pictures furiously, while I ran

our boat in circles and figure eights in the area of the factory ship. Much of her crew, it seemed, was occupied in the flensing operation, stripping the skin and blubber from the whales. Blood coursed down the deck and into the sea, and sharks were everywhere. Some crew members lined the deck railing, taking pictures and pointing at us. They laughed and jabbered, as if watching a circus.

Suddenly, without thinking, I threw the throttle wide open. My cameramen nearly popped out of the boat when we hit, at full speed. From a short way out, I had climbed the back of a whale being pulled tail first up the chute at the stern of the *Dalniy Vostok*.

"Maybe this will stop you!" I screamed up to the flensing deck. But it was a totally useless gesture.

We teetered precariously atop the whale before sliding back into the water. For a moment, as we hung on the back of the enormous carcass, our outboard engine's propeller spun madly in the open air. And then we were bouncing among the waves again. The *Dalniy Vostok* crewmen never missed a beat. The cable attached to the whale pulled its prey inexorably up the chute and onto the deck. There, the workmen turned the remains into raw materials.

I saw the V-shaped Avon heading for the *James Bay*, and it seemed to be the time for us to go back, too. Aboard the Avon, Eileen Chivers had thought to take along some gifts—whale pins, Greenpeace T-shirts, a bottle of *Johnny Walker* scotch whiskey—and these she had passed up to crewmen aboard one of the killer ships. They, in turn, had handed down Russian cigarettes and scurried about looking for other reciprocities. But an order from the bridge ended the gift-swapping.

After stowing our inflatables aboard the *James Bay*,

we unlimbered our yard-wide loudspeakers and aimed them at the *Dalniy Vostok*. Crew members stood around quietly on deck as some of our people made appeals to stop the whaling—Bob Hunter in English, Captain Korotva in Russian and Czech, Tanaka in Japanese, Mary Lee in French, and David Garrick in Spanish—and then, all of a sudden, the big ship increased its speed from about five knots to fifteen and changed its heading from due west to north-northwest. We chased along, keeping up even when the *Dalniy Vostok* kicked up to eighteen knots.

"That captain," Korotva said. "He's taking us away from Honolulu so we can't go in for a quick refueling. He can refuel at sea, with tankers. But we have to go somewhere. And if he makes us go a long way, he gets us out of his hair."

We chased the *Dalniy Vostok* for forty hours. At eighteen knots, our gauges were plummeting, and we no longer had any choice. We had to head for Honolulu. At 11 P.M. on July 20, 1976, we broke off from the Soviet whaling fleet and made a lazy 180-degree turn.

We spent eighteen days in Hawaii. For many in our crew, it was the first visit to that fabled land of orchids and pineapples. But we had a heavy schedule of serious matters to attend to. First, we attacked our perennial problem of funds for fuel and supplies. We sold Greenpeace T-shirts and other souvenirs, talked to newspaper and radio-television reporters, and accepted all the practical and finanical help we could get to refit the *James Bay* for another sortie. We debated whether to head west and seek out the Japanese whalers in the farther reaches of the Pacific, or to stay with the Soviets. In the end, we chose the devil we knew: We would find the Soviets again as we worked our way back to Vancouver.

Before we left Hawaii, I had an experience with a dolphin that convinced me once and for all that we must pursue the study of interspecies communication. We have not yet even begun to scratch the surface, or even to comprehend the possibilities of communicating with these mammals.

By a stroke of luck, I was invited to go swimming at a Honolulu aquarium where there was a female dolphin named Puka, and we spent more than two hours cavorting together. She tested me at first, shoving and butting and trying to bite. But, when I nudged her and pushed her away, she became gentler and friendlier. She was playful with George Korotva and Ross Thornwood, too, but indifferent to the others in our group. The more physical we were and the less timid, the more she seemed to like us.

Puka seemed particularly to like being dragged backwards by the tail, being thrown completely out of the water by the tail, and being rolled over and over, for she always came back for more after we did these things. And she indicated in the same way that she enjoyed having her belly and the area below her pectoral fins tickled, as well as swimming with me when my arm was around her, playing chase and charge, and swimming belly to belly with me. The more physical the play, the pinker her belly became.

We moved from our berthing near Pearl Harbor to Kauai and then to Lahaina, Maui, with one brief run at the Japanese in between. This consisted of staying at Lahaina, to conserve fuel, while we monitored aerial reconnaissance reports made available to us on the movements of the 518-foot *Kyokuyo Maru 3* and seven harpoon ships working about five hundred miles northwest of Honolulu near French Frigate Shoals. But some of our group felt that not enough came of this effort to make an all-out attack worth our while. I left the ship in Maui, returned to Vancouver, and flew to Norway to attend the Marine Mammal Conference in Bergen. So I was not on board when the decision was made to go after the Russians again.

That decision brought no great joy, I am sure, to the captain of the *Dalniy Vostok* as, for the third time in little more than a year, he stood on his bridge and watched the *James Bay* come sailing up to complicate his life. At first, he made a run for it, trying to shake his pursuers, but then settled into a gentler pace.

It became, in fact, something of a gentleman's game. The killer ships of the *Dalniy Vostok* never fired their harpoons if inflatables and photographers were on the scene. They did manage to bring in some kills, however, by making them over the horizon, out of sight and range. It was costly in fuel to keep up the chase, day after day, but those aboard the *James Bay* felt they were being effective in saving whales, if only temporarily.

There was a terrible scare on August 22, a Sunday. A soupy fog enveloped the whaling fleet, the *James Bay*, and two inflatables that were then in the water for the purpose of taking pictures and blocking harpoon shots. Afterward, crewman Mike Bailey recalled: "The fog caught us completely off guard." And Susi Leger, whose boat had drifted so far away that she could no longer hear the fog horn of the *James Bay*, said the Russians saw her in trouble but "just pulled away, leaving us behind." Finally, just as the smothering blanket began to lift to about five hundred feet, the two little boats bobbed back in view, their occupants composed but considerably subdued.

On Sunday, September 6, 1976, the *James Bay* sailed back into Vancouver, fuel gauge down but flags flying, bodies sagging but spirits soaring. Some three thousand of the faithful were on the docks at Jericho Beach, cheering lustily.

7

Return to Labrador

OUR STILL PICTURES OF the Canadian and Norwegian "swilers" and the harp seals appeared in publications around the globe. Our movies were being shown in Canada, the United States, England, and all the countries of Western Europe. Protests, particularly against scenes of the seals being skinned alive, were pouring in to the governments of Canada and Norway. In one week alone, Ottawa received more than five thousand letters. The Canadian government began talking of counter-measures, even ordering up a film of its own to try to justify the hunt. In Washington, protesters marched against plans to "harvest" some of the northern fur seals in Alaska's Pribilof Islands, and spokesmen for the United States fur industry grumbled about "a campaign of vilification against the fur trade."

It was in this context that we prepared our second foray onto the ice off Newfoundland, against the harp seal hunt of 1977. I was the expedition leader, and I chose Al Johnson as deputy leader. We all worked harder than ever through the Greenpeace Foundation, of which I was by then a director, to raise funds to help finance our projected new harassment of the sealers and to pay off the debts of past expeditions. We relied heav-

ily on propaganda to build public support and raise
funds; the Canadian government was not idle on that
front, either. Fisheries Minister Romeo LeBlanc
engaged us in a running battle of charges and counter-
charges, and, on the scene, the Newfoundland government voted six thousand dollars in grants to local organizations that vowed to oppose us (at least twenty
already were formed). The uneasy alliance we had
struck the previous year with the Newfoundland fishermen union fell apart. Richard Cashin, president of
the union, accused us of reneging on a commitment the
year before to support local landsmen's right to "swile."
The Greenpeace board of directors had made that
commitment. I had rescinded it, using my authority as
expedition leader. For Cashin's benefit, Greenpeace put
out a statement that said in part: "We will oppose the
seal hunt by anyone who hunts seals."

We rejected as nonsense the Canadian and Newfoundland governments' arguments that no other
employment was available to the men who killed baby
harp seals each spring. We cited the Canadian government's own statistics showing that "swiling" constituted
only one-third of the Newfoundlanders' income, and
that $5 million to $6 million was spent each year to support an industry that brought in a total of only about 13
million (the government's estimate of the annual trade
in the pups' white pelts).

We found some encouraging words elsewhere. The
Canadian government's own study commission in 1972
had called for a "phasing out of the Canadian and Norwegian harp and hood seal hunt" as a conservation measure. And the celebrated American biologist, Victor B.
Scheffer, told us that people were becoming more
aware of the cruelty and senselessness of the seal hunt.

However, he warned that the killing of seals will continue "as long as world opinion assigns a high priority to their commercial use," and he added, "But I hope that world opinion will change, that present values and goals will increasingly be questioned, and that living seals will one day be valued above dead ones."

Despite our best efforts, though, the Canadian government, in consultation with the government of Norway, set a quota of 170,000 for the 1977 kill. Incredibly, that was higher than the previous year, even though moratoriums had been called for, not only by groups such as ours, but by the Canadian government's own study committee. The 170,000 harp seals to be slaughtered would include 6,000 adults and 12,000 "subadults" (those below five years, the age at which females normally first produce), as well as 152,000 "whitecoats" under six weeks old. Despite much lower estimates from conservation groups, the Canadian government decided arbitrarily that there were 1.2 million harp seals altogether, with 330,000 pups expected in March 1977. This was almost twice as high as the birth rate forecast by such nonpartisan authorities as Dr. David Sergeant and biologists at Guelph University in Ontario who had conducted a detailed aerial reconnaissance. The Guelph scientists had also noted that the harp seals were bearing pups at an earlier age, and they interpreted this as an instinctive effort to combat a declining population—a sign that hunting pressures on the herd might be approaching the level of unacceptability.

Guelph veterinarians conducted other studies the results of which we seized on in our propaganda struggle with Ottawa (where, incidentally, we felt we had scored something of a coup when Prime Minister

Pierre Trudeau's wife, Margaret, announced that, henceforth, she would "never wear a baby seal"). One Guelph study was aimed at discovering what would happen to seals if they should be subjected to a large oil spill. The answer would be important to the burgeoning government-controlled oil industry in Canada, and it is not clear that there was ever any intention of making the findings public.

The Vancouver *Sun* obtained a copy of one of the reports arising from the research, however, and published a story based on it in early 1976. It showed that some seals died when covered with oil and others when force-fed doses of crude oil. Survivors of these tests were shot or clubbed to death so that their bodies could be examined in post-mortem operations to determine the effects of the experiments. All told, according to the report, more than a hundred harp and ringed seals were used, of whom few survived. An additional sixty-four died during efforts to capture them with nets for use in the tests.

Joseph R. Geraci, a spokesman for the college, denounced the article as "distorted and, in some cases, out of context"—a standard denial which, however, never denied the findings of the study (the *Sun,* after all, was in possession of the report itself).

Geraci said the experimenters were surprised when three seals died after being placed in a holding pool covered with a one-centimeter film of oil. He told the Vancouver *Sun:*

"They died within seventy-one minutes—a response we didn't expect to find. In open water, the same treatment had no long-lasting effects.

"We found that seals under stress, whether by captivity, molting, parasitism or naturally occurring diseases, or in times of low food production, are more susceptible to these changes."

Our public relations campaign brought us mixed blessings from abroad. One person whose interest we attracted in a big way was a Swiss toymaker named Franz Weber, whose activities on behalf of conservation and consumer interests were so many and so varied that European journalists had taken to calling him "the Ralph Nader of Europe." The forty-nine-year-old Weber, who had been a newsman before making a fortune in toy manufacturing, was a brilliant promoter. He telephoned us and wrote us, insisting he wanted to be present when we protested the 1977 harp seal hunt. Weber was bubbling over with energy and ideas, and we welcomed that, but his tactics sometimes were so flamboyant that, in the end, they proved counter-productive among the more conservative elements we were trying to reach and impress. It was Weber who eventually brought along Brigitte Bardot (also a mixed blessing) and financed the flight of European journalists to the hunt (one of whom showed up wearing his mother's fur coat), assuring us considerable friendly coverage. But it was also Weber who ignited local antipathy long before we reached Newfoundland with a grandiose scheme to have the people there drop the hunt in exchange for: 1. $400,000 cash, 2. his setting up a fake fur coat factory in the area, 3. his sparking a tourist trade that would feature dogsled trips to the ice so that people could see the seals, and 4. all or part of about one million dollars that Weber and his artist-wife Judith, had cleared the Christmas before from the sale of their toy seals.

However wild Weber's ideas struck some people, I was intrigued. I flew to Montreux in Switzerland, talked with the Webers, and returned to Vancouver to push for his factory proposal. It would not take much employment to match the few hundred dollars the New-foundland sealers made from their killing per season, and so Weber's scheme could be one way of destroying the government's argument that the men needed the work. For Weber's part, he said our 1976 campaign had inspired him and his wife to design and mass-produce the synthetic toy seals, and he wanted to use their profits to help halt the slaughter.

"It's been a crazy success all over Europe, this little seal, and at twelve dollars each," Weber told me. "In Switzerland alone, we sold twenty thousand for Christmas. We want to have grand campaigns of sales and publicity in the United States, and in Japan, too. Each person who buys a toy seal is a person who is mobilized and militant for our crusade. The more we sell, the more people we have on our side. We will represent millions of people in the world—a grand force!"

We were used to a hand-to-mouth existence, so that kind of talk sounded sweet. Even if nothing came of it, Weber's bouncing optimism was good for the spirit. Although his talk of flying over scores of journalists and housing them in moored ships because there were not enough hotel rooms available sounded wildly improbable, it started me thinking. Why not buy or lease a ship for our anti-hunt activities—an icebreaker, perhaps? With helicopters, we had speed and mobility, but weather was quick to ground them. With an icebreaker, we would be on a par with the sealing ships that could operate in the worst blizzard while we huddled helplessly in our wind-whipped tents at Belle Isle or some other haven. It was something to think about.

Predictably, Canadian Fisheries Minister Roméo

LeBlanc rejected Weber's offer of money and employment for the Newfoundlanders. And just as predictably,
we attacked LeBlanc. I wrote in *Greenpeace Chronicles:*

What the Minister seems to forget is that he must also represent the wishes and interests of the thousands of Canadians
opposed to this annual slaughter. . . . Our requests for meetings are not answered.

If the Minister is truly interested in the financial circum-
stances of the sealers, he would not have turned down the
$2.5 million offer of compensation by Mr. Franz Weber of
Switzerland. He would not have scoffed at Mr. Weber's offer
to build a fake-fur factory in Newfoundland which would
employ 600 Newfoundlanders as compared with the present
150 commercial sealers from the same province. Year-round
employment vs. seasonal employment, and the government
turned it down!

Just what are M. LeBlanc's motivations? Just who is it that
profits from this hunt?

Canada spends more money policing the hunt than Canadian citizens make from it. There is a very fishy smell clinging
to the Ministry of Fisheries and the Environment. Many
Canadians and people of other nations are tired of holding
their noses.

Our 1976 campaign was bearing fruit elsewhere
abroad. In England, that land of animal lovers, the London *Sunday Times* and the *Guardian* of Manchester produced articles giving both sides of the story, but, we
thought, evidencing somewhat of a tilt in our favor. The
British contingent of the International Fund for Animal
Welfare announced a demonstration parade against the
seal hunt culminating at Canada House in London on
the date of the start of the killing (March 12, although
fierce weather off Newfoundland forced a delay).

A huge billboard appeared off Trafalgar Square

across from Canada House. Set up for a month by the 3,500-member British branch of the International Fund, it cost $1,500. It showed a heroic-sized picture of a man bending over in the act of clubbing a dewy-eyed "whitecoat," and it shouted in big block letters:

CANADA'S SHAME

We welcomed this, as we welcomed all support, for the Canadian government was beating its own drumfire of propaganda as the mid-March start of the hunt approached. Aside from the recurring theme of economic necessity, the cultural-heritage-romance argument kept coming out of Ottawa, and we fought back with raw figures.

Most authorities agreed with the following summary by Fred Bruemmer, a writer and conservationist who has studied the two hundred years of the decimation of the harp seal herds and assiduously avoids taking sides in the controversy:

"The hunt of the harp seals has no equal. It has been going on for nearly two hundred years, and more than fifty million seals have been killed in the [Labrador] Front and Gulf [of St. Lawrence] herds of Newfoundland alone. If one adds to this the harp seals killed from the other two herds—the one east of Greenland, the other in Russia's White Sea—the total rises to about seventy million, the greatest, most protracted mass slaughter ever inflicted upon any wild mammal species."

The Greenpeace Foundation, meanwhile, was undergoing what might be called, for lack of a better description, a severe case of growing pains. We had some eighty thousand members, according to our records, but we were miserably in debt, and the leadership in Vancouver seemed to be bogged down in bickering over who should hold what office and who should be in charge of this and that, and so on. It seemed to me we were in danger of becoming an internal debating society and losing sight of what we had organized for: effective, dramatic protest.

The Foundation's headquarters office was in a state of chronic confusion, with records lying about in the open except at the times one needed them. I was delighted, therefore, to go to the office one day and find a young woman hard at work trying to bring order out of the chaos. She was young and pretty, dedicated to the cause of animal preservation, and inordinately articulate and informed on the subject. I tried not to show it, but I was enchanted.

Her name was Starlet Lum and she came from a large Chinese-American family whose roots in Vancouver could be traced back for several generations. Like most Oriental families I had come to know in Vancouver, the Lums were close-knit, polite, and respectful— and fiercely loyal. In Starlet, I could see these qualities as well.

I resolved to see more of her, and I did. At the office, we worked together on projects associated with the 1977 seal hunt, and we ate together, went for walks and to the movies together, and spent a lot of time talking about our lives and our hopes and ambitions. Anybody with any sense could see that we were falling in love. I wanted her along on the seal expedition in some capacity. Because she speaks French, I assigned her to Montreal, to handle the news media operations there.

Thirteen of us left by train from Vancouver on Monday, March 7, 1977. We would be joined by another dozen or so along the way or when we arrived on the east coast. Deputy expedition leader Al Johnson set the tone, summing up our intentions in a departure statement:

"This year we're going to do our best physically to stop the hunt. Some of us may not be coming back. It's getting to the point where we have to make a stand. This is the year we have to do it. If we don't, the harp seal will soon be just a memory."

Besides Al and me, our group included Peter Ballem, Bruce Bunting, George Potter, Cory Stiller, Marvin Tanasychuk, Alan Thornton, Laurent Trudel, and Gary Zimmerman, plus three young women from Norway: Vibeke Arvidsson of Bergen, and Kristin Aarflot and Elisabeth Rasmusson of Oslo. We were truly international, with members from Canada, Britain, Norway, and the United States.

The three Norwegian women had come to meet me in Bergen, when I was the Greenpeace delegate to the 1976 Marine Mammal Conference. Ever since, they had been working for us and saving up for this trip. They hoped to talk to the Norwegian sealers and persuade them to stop the hunt. At the least, they would help track the Norwegian ships by monitoring their radio traffic. The three spoke flawless English.

The Vancouver *Sun* gave us a sprightly sendoff. Newspapers in Edmonton and Montreal were attentive, too, and we were delighted to capture such attention. There was the possibility that we could die on the ice this time—we said so over and over, which was not only good propaganda but probably also insurance of a sort against our getting quietly done in—and we wanted to take advantage of whatever space the news media would provide. The *Sun,* in an editorial harking back to an earlier article that had called us "noxious twits," gave us a backhanded compliment for our ability to call attention to our work, adding good-naturedly:

Russian harpoon boat threatens Paul Watson and Marilyn Kaga for interfering with its whaling operations in 1976.

REX WEYLER PHOTO

Watson, in inflatable dinghy, photographs the harpoon boat transferring its kill to the factory ship *Dalniy Vostok*.

REX WEYLER PHOTO

Above: Paul Watson measures a dead baby whale, a victim of the Russians, and finds it below the legal limit. REX WEYLER PHOTO

Below, left: Paul Watson has handcuffed himself to the winch line of a sealing ship to interrupt the seal harvest, 1977. PETER BELLAM PHOTO

Below, right: Tony, Paul Watson's father, serves as cook on the 1979 expedition to save the harp seals. MARY BLOOM PHOTO

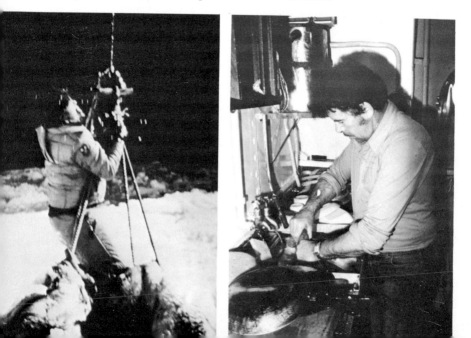

Above: Watson and crew member Star-let Lum—the two were later married.

MARY BLOOM PHOTO

Below: Crew members go to work with shovels and pickaxes to free the ice-bound *Sea Shepherd* in 1979. MARY BLOOM PHOTO

At right: Paul Watson climbing the *Sea Shepherd*'s mast. MARY BLOOM PHOTO

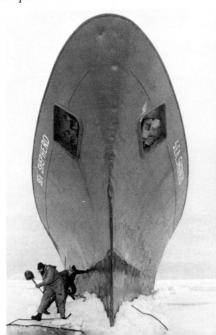

The pirate whaler *Sierra,* after being rammed by the *Sea Shepherd* off Portugal in July, 1979. MARCUS HALEVI PHOTO

Left to right: Peter Woof, Paul Watson, and Jerry Doran on board *Sea Shepherd* after crippling the *Sierra.* MARCUS HALEVI PHOTO

Crew members of *Sea Shepherd* celebrate their victory over the *Sierra. Left to right:* Stanley Jackson, Alex Oacheco, Paul Watson, Gail Lima (*head of table*), Al Indelicato (*partially hidden*), Giovanni Tondi, Margaret Morey of the Fund for Animals, South African journalist Neil Jacobson, William Shober, and David Sellers. MARCUS HALEVI PHOTO

On New Year's Eve, 1979, Watson and others scuttled *Sea Shepherd* to save the vessel from being impounded by the Portuguese government. ASSOCIATED PRESS, LONDON, PHOTO

Watson and crew members are arraigned in Quebec on charges of interfering with the seal hunt. That same day, February 6, 1980, the *Sierra* was sunk in Lisbon harbor. MARCUS HALEVI PHOTO

The overturned hull of the *Sierra* after the ship was blown up. ASSOCIATED PRESS, LONDON, PHOTO

Starlet Lum-Watson with daughter, Lilliolani.

"A worthy cause, too, if it brings us a step closer to the day when man no longer finds it necessary to kill his fellow creatures for fun or profit.

"Bon voyage, noxious twits."

Our cause had also stirred some official interest south of the border. Rep. Leo Ryan (D-California) engineered adoption by the U.S. House of Representatives of a resolution condemning Canada's and Norway's killing of baby harp seals as "cruel practice." He went to Newfoundland the next year, on a fact-finding trip.

This was the same Rep. Ryan who had voluntarily spent time in prison so that he could study first hand the need for reforms. And, unhappily, it was the same Rep. Ryan who, in 1978, was slain in the mass murder–

suicides ordered by the Reverend James Jones at Jones-
town, near Georgetown, Guyana, in South America.

Ryan's resolution, keyed to his determination that
the seal herds would disappear unless the killings
stopped, was received in Newfoundland with conster-
nation and indignation. Roy Pilgrim, chairman of the
citizens group opposing protesters in the community of
St. Anthony, snapped, "They don't know what they're
talking about." Others objected that the Americans were
guilty of undue interference, but Rep. Ryan, in defend-
ing the action, said it was the duty of the U.S. House of
Representatives "to be concerned about matters of
world-wide importance that affect our lives on this
planet."

As the tempo of the impending confrontation quick-
ened, the Royal Canadian Mounted Police assigned
fifty-five mounties to the hunt. Ostensibly, their mission
was to keep order. But the suspicion on both sides was
that they would support the hunt and put down the
objectors, perhaps even arrest them with a show of
force. We all braced for a hard time.

As before, we planned to use helicopters for sorties
out to the ice—three this time instead of two. We set up
a base headquarters in the tiny community of Blanc
Sablon in Quebec on the Strait of Belle Isle that sepa-
rates Newfoundland from Labrador. This gave us a
central position from which to fly to the Gulf and out to
the floating Front. Our forward base would again be
Belle Isle, about thirty miles north of St. Anthony. We
used a single-engined monoplane, an Otter, to ferry
fuel and supplies to our field camp on the barren island
of ice and rock about twenty miles off the coast of
Labrador. The ice looked thin, broken up, dangerous.
We saw few seals, and we wondered if the devastation

of the herds had already caused a visible reduction in population.

Brigitte Bardot flew in with her entourage—Franz Weber, a three-man television team to make a documentary film of her visit, an organizer, a still-photographer, and her boy friend, Mirko, plus two pilots for the Lear jet. Their first stop, after a fourteen-hour flight from Le Bourget in Paris, was Sept Iles in Quebec. Despite the hour (2:30 A.M.), she came off the plane with her propaganda guns blazing.

"The whole world has risen up against the baby seal hunt," she declared, "and Canada runs the risk of diplomatic conflicts if the situation doesn't change. Seals belong to the national heritage. Canada must stop the massacre because, at the current rate, the last of the seals will be finished by 1985."

The next day (Tuesday, March 15, 1977), Bardot was welcomed to the seal hunt in Blanc Sablon by Royal Canadian Mounted Police. They slapped a two hundred dollar fine on her Lear jet, as a sort of parking ticket, calling it a violation of a "customs technicality." Bryan Davies was having legal-technicality problems, too. Davies, flying his own helicopter, was grounded on four charges of violating the sealing regulations, allegedly by flying lower than two thousand feet above a seal and landing less than one-half nautical mile from a seal.

Bardot's life in the movie world and on her farm near Paris did not prepare her for the hardships and bitter cold of seal country. She tried during her stay to get in touch with Prime Minister Pierre Trudeau in Ottawa, but he was always otherwise occupied and unavailable. She held a news conference in St. Anthony, amid a circus atmosphere of rude reporters snickering and elbowing each other, and, like a schoolmarm, had to yell, "Silence!" to maintain order. She went out on the ice on her own at one point, and, by her account, picked up and cuddled a baby seal—another technical violation, as the law says the seals may not be moved. I flew her as our guest to visit our forward camp at Belle Isle. But it seemed to me she wanted only to coo over a beautiful white baby seal. She looked seasick and cringed when, at her St. Anthony news conference, somebody tried to get her to pose with the dead but still-warm body of a baby seal in a plastic bag.

Meantime, we got ready to make our run. From St. Anthony, our three Jetranger helicopters whirred in to Belle Isle to pick us up for the flight out to the floes. Moments later, our bright orange Otter dipped down to a hazardous landing on the uneven terrain. The engine roared and slowly wound down, the propeller spun to a halt, and the door opened. Out stepped a dozen European journalists, looking pale and shaken as they crowded around Al Johnson for a briefing. The last man out of the Otter was the pilot, a jolly, mustachioed Quebecois who seemed always to be smiling and who told us he would be happy to fly us out to the ice himself but he could not find a floe big enough to land on. The ice was more broken and therefore more dangerous than it had been the previous year.

"Our intentions," Al Johnson said, revealing our strategy for the first time, "are to attempt to shut down a sealing vessel. We are prepared to put our lives in jeopardy by placing our bodies in their way, between club and seal and before and behind the ship itself.

"The future of an entire species is at stake. Ultimately, the future of our own species is at stake. We must take the step of committing ourselves to this serious and drastic effort to interfere."

We headed east in our helicopters, the sky overhead a piercing blue, but the ice below an ominous maze of floes that, even from two thousand feet, looked threatening. In about a half-hour, the eleven Norwegian and Canadian sealing ships came into view, each of them trailing a ribbon of scarlet on either side. My stomach heaved, as it had the year before, at the sight of that red blood against the icy blue.

It was almost 9:30 in the morning when we circled, checking to make sure there were no seals in the area, and landed on the biggest ice pan we could find that was at least a half-mile from the slaughtering. We picked a pan about forty feet wide more than two miles away from the nearest sealing ship. It was like landing on a raft. The pan bobbed and weaved in an eight-foot swell, and we had the unreal feeling of stepping off the helicopter into a major earthquake. The second helicopter put down on the same floe. But the third was forced to land on a pan about a hundred yards away. It would appear and reappear with the rise and fall of each swell. The thought of hopping from shifting floe to shifting floe for two miles terrified me, but I knew it was dangerous to dwell on that for very long.

"Everybody out!" I yelled. "Let's go!"

Eleven of us had started. A photographer for *Time* magazine, who had assured me he could take the rigors of the ice because he had been steeled in Vietnam, refused to leave the helicopter. He bet me ten dollars I would not survive (I looked him up and collected later). Another photographer stayed aboard, too, making us nine on the ice.

By half-past noon, we had only five in our party: Alan Thornton, from Greenpeace England; Peter Ballem, a Vancouver lawyer who was our legal adviser;

Fred Easton, our cameraman; Michael Chechik, our soundman; and myself. The elements robbed us of four: Al Johnson sprained his ankle on one jump between floes, and he hobbled back to the choppers with our documentary photographer and two crew members, all suffering from exhaustion. By my reckoning, at that point we were about halfway to the ships.

Suddenly, we realized we were among the seals, and once more I was struck by the beauty of the babies. Canadian Fisheries Minister Roméo LeBlanc had once chortled that it was the beauty of the baby seals that aroused my interest, not any humanitarian instinct to prevent carnage. That charge of his came back to me as I looked about at the "whitecoats" on the ice, and I thought of a rejoinder: "But the only reason they are killed is because they are so beautiful!"

The noises they were making were the happy sounds of new life. We were still far from the killing grounds, and there was an air of quiet security. The mother seals watched us warily, but there was no alarm.

And then, to my left, I picked up a cry that was somewhat more insistent than all the others, with an edge of fear to it. I went over and looked around. I saw that two ice pans had moved apart and a pup had fallen into the crack. These babies, with their underdeveloped tails and flippers, cannot swim, and this particular one was floundering about in the frigid water, trying desperately to climb up the edge, but it was too high for him. The ice pans were moving back together and it seemed certain he would be crushed.

I dropped my backpack and rushed to the opening. With inches to spare, I grabbed him by a flipper and pulled him to safety. I gave his little head a pat and stepped back.

The pup aimed his nose at the sky, like a wolf in full bay, and let out a mournful cry. He looked like any other lost creature, bewildered and unable to cope on his own. On the other side of the pan a female appeared. She flopped quickly to the pup's side, gave me a quizzical look, and, turning, led her baby away.

By mid-afternoon, with about a half-hour of floe-jumping to go before we reached the ships, we had to make a decision. By law and for safety's sake, the helicopters had to be off the ice before dark. That meant we had to break off our sortie or stay on the ice all night. We were all thirsty and tired. Our legs were sore and our faces were raw from sunburn caused by glare off the ice. We wondered whether to ditch the inflatable boat we had been dragging along with us, a dead weight most of the time but exceedingly useful for crossing the "leads" between the ice pans. We decided to hang on to the inflatable, and, by vote, agreed unanimously to stay on the ice, even though the miserable cold might kill some or all of us.

Shortly after 3 P.M. we reached the killing ground. Blood was on the ice everywhere. As before, the babies were crying, but their shrieks were full of fear, and they often would end abruptly in the dull *thwack!* of the bat.

The first sealer we met was a big man. His hands and face were plastered with the rusty crust of dried blood, and his clothes looked black with gore. As I appeared, he was bending over a pup, knife in hand. His club was lying on the ice behind him. The sealer looked up. I could see no eyes, only the image of the bloody scene in his big, reflecting sunglasses.

As the sealer bent to his task, assiduously ignoring me and quickly carving the pelt from the warm little body, I walked slowly behind him. I picked up his club and decorously, almost ceremoniously, I threw it into an open lead. Unfortunately, it floated. But the sealer would have to retrieve it.

The next sealer I saw was in a quandary. He was dragging a pelt attached by a rope to a pile of pelts that was being arranged for retrieval by the ship. To get to where he was headed, he had to jump from the ice pan he was on to the one next to it. But Alan Thornton was sitting in the only spot he could jump to safely. The sealer hesitated, pondering. Then he obviously decided to jump to another floe nearby—a more difficult leap. Before taking off, he threw the end of his rope to this floe. And just before he landed, I reached over and yanked his rope back to the floe he had just left. He was no better off than he had been before. I moved on, leaving Al Thornton sitting there staring at the sealer like Edgar Allan Poe's raven.

In a few minutes, two helicopters came hedgehopping across the ice, at about fifteen feet over the heads of the seals. We could see a half-dozen Fisheries Ministry officers getting out when they landed, and it seemed we were about to be arrested. All of us raced to the sealing ship *Martin Karlsen,* determined to make a try at halting her operations before the lawmen took us away.

Alan Thornton went to the rear and I took up a position at the bow. The ship kept plowing ahead, pushing ice pans up and away. Alan had gotten the inflatable into the water to block any effort at backing up, and I stood on the unsteady floe that was about one hundred feet ahead of the *Martin Karlsen.* And still she came, the cold red bow growing taller and taller. The ice beneath my feet shuddered as she hit the floe I was on. I stumbled but I did not fall. And then I realized that I was being pushed along. We moved that way for about thirty feet, being swept aside at last to drift past the hull on the starboard side. On deck, two dozen sealers at the rail jeered and made obscene hand gestures. I waved and yelled at my people to stand fast.

The *Martin Karlsen* stopped about a hundred yards away to pick up a pile of pelts. I watched some sealers hook up a winch cable to the pelts. The line was paid out from the starboard side and over the ice to the skins.

An idea flashed. It seemed to me I had a foolproof way to shut down the ship, at least for a while. I signaled to my crew, and we all headed for the pelts.

As I approached, four Newfoundlanders at the end of the cable stopped their work and stepped back. They seemed to be under orders to let us harangue them if that is what we meant to do. But my plan was entirely different. I had no intention of wasting time talking.

Before leaving Belle Isle, I had attached a pair of handcuffs to my belt, and, as I walked up to the winch cable and its load of sealskins, I fumbled for them. With a quick flick of the wrist, I attached myself with the cuffs to the line.

The Newfoundland sealers stared at me speechless. From the deck, where the men at the rails could see this tableau, came a chant, "Haul t'b'y in!" and, "Give t'b'y a right cold swim!"

I felt elated. Surely, I thought, the ship was unable to proceed. Now the captain would have to hold up the operation until he could figure out a way to detach me from the pelts and the winch cable. And then I heard the sealer beside me mutter:

"Ye are right daft, b'y! We's will kill ya, f'sure!"

My heart almost stopped when I felt the first tug. The cable went taut. The sealers aboard cheered and yelled encouragement to the winch operator, and he responded.

I was yanked off my feet and pulled across the ice.

My pants and parka ripped on the sharp edges. The ice disappeared and I was in a thick sludge of ice and water, and it was very cold.

The cable whipped upward, pulling me clear of the surface. I sailed through the air and slammed into the hull of the ship. The winch spun some more, and the pelts and I were about ten feet above the water. The line stopped and then slackened, dropping me into the water waist-deep, stopping with a jerk. Immediately, the line tightened and I was clear of the water again, only to be dropped again, this time neck-deep. Once more, the winch whined, and up I went into the air, to be doused a third time. I was a mouse on a string. After the fourth dunk, when the winch stopped just as I reached the top, the strain broke my belt, and I tumbled into the icy water.

The shock immobilized me. I could not move my legs. My arms were going numb, too. My chest felt on fire. Paralyzed, without much sense of what I could do, I bobbed to the surface. With my head craned back, I could see the deck.

"For God's sake," I yelled. "Throw me a rope!"

The sealers at the rail jeered and made a thumbs-down gesture. I heard one of them call out:

"Drown, ya bloody bastard!"

I closed my eyes. There was no pain. There was, in fact, not much of anything, only the fading jeers and a sense of approaching peace.

There was a faint pressure on my shoulder. I opened my eyes to see Peter Ballem and Al Thornton hovering over me. They seemed to be trying to get me out of the water and into our rubber raft. Silence came, and then darkness.

When I opened my eyes again, I was surprised to find myself still on the ice. I could see Al slapping my legs, but I felt nothing. Peter was arguing with a Fisheries Ministry officer, who kept shouting that he had no authority to order the captain to take me aboard. I seemed to be falling in and out of consciousness for an incredibly long time, but I was told later it was only a half-hour.

There was movement again, a jostling, and I awoke to find myself strapped into a stretcher with lifting lines attached to it. Peter was holding the stretcher back, as some sealers, pulling on other lines, sought to drag the stretcher through the water before hoisting it up the side of the hull. In the scuffle, Peter fell into the water. I managed to grab him by an arm, and Alan helped him back onto the ice.

At the ship's gunwale, the stretcher stopped. Six sealers took hold of it and turned it over, but the straps kept me from falling out. I could not fall out, but neither could I move enough to defend myself. One of the sealers grabbed me by the hair and shouted into my ear:

"We's a-going t'give ya a good taste of swile fat, b'y!"

With that, he and the others pushed my face into the bloody seal blubber. I could not breathe. I realized that I was suffocating. They were still yelling in my ear.

"Suffocate, y'bleeding do-gooder!"

"Shove a pelt down his damn throat!"

After what seemed an eternity, somebody I took to be the first officer came up and ordered a halt. The men were still raging, though, and, as I was dragged away by the rope through the blood and seal fat on the deck, they crowded around and aimed kicks at me.

These landed with a dull thud each time as the heavy sealer's boots found my legs and side. I could feel them through the numbness, and I wondered whether I had not been better off in the water.

At the door to a cabin somewhere on the officers'

deck, I was dumped in a heap. My wet clothing was removed and a blanket thrown over me. I was alone with a Fisheries Ministry officer and the first mate until Peter Ballem argued his way on board. Alan Thornton had fought to come to my aid, too, but, when a sealer swung a club at him, he lost his hold on the side of the ship and fell to an ice pan. Injured, he was flown out to St. Anthony in one of our helicopters, which had been given special permission for this purpose.

That evening, as Peter and I sat in the officer's cabin assigned us, feeling rather like prisoners, a knock came on the door. It was the ship's captain. He looked us over for a brief moment, and, without further ceremony, went straight to the point.

"What the hell are you trying to pull?" he asked. "Trying to get yourself killed? For what? For a damn seal? It ain't worth it, boy."

I started in to explain that, unless people like me take drastic actions, there may be no more harp seals, and I began to cite the statistics of declining seal population. But he had not come to listen.

"People like you are a menace," he said. "There are more seals now than ever before. Don't tell me, boy. I've been sealing all my life. Your kind put an end to whaling, and now the ocean is overrun with whales, eating all our fish. It's all politics.

"I used to be a whaler. Now, I'm just a sealer.

"The whole damn lot of you do-gooders can go straight to hell."

With that, he turned on his heel and walked out.

I spent a restless night, my body burning and aching. The sun shining through the porthole woke me up at 6:30 A.M. on that second day of the hunt—March 16, 1977—and, when I opened the porthole, I could hear the cries of the dying seals. Seals were all around us, mothers and babies, and the ship was moving through the ice dropping large groups of sealers in a great circle. Peter and I waited impatiently to leave, miserable in the midst of all the killing.

Finally, shortly before noon, our helicopter came. We left the hell ship as fast as we could. We noticed, as we left, that another helicopter was there, too, dropping off Royal Canadian Mounted Police guards at the ships. What were these armed guards there to do? Protect the ships against us unarmed pacifists?

From the *Martin Karlsen* we went by helicopter to Blanc Sabon in Quebec, where I checked into a hospital. My body temperature was two degrees below normal and I was in quite a bit of pain. As it turned out, I had pneumonia, and the hospital put me to bed.

David Garrick led a crew of eight on the ice, meanwhile, operating against the sealer *Theron*. But the weather was closing in, making flying conditions impossible over the next few days. The hardy crew at the Belle Isle forward base stuck it out until March 20, but by then there was little sense in staying on. The Labrador Front had moved out of our range, and we were running out of money, anyway, and so, on March 21, we announced that the 1977 anti-sealing expedition was formally at an end.

The worst day for me was that last one aboard the *Martin Karlsen* as Peter Ballem and I waited to be taken off by helicopter. For four hours we watched the killing. I saw nearly three hundred baby seals die. Some fell beneath the clubs, others were run down by the sealing ship as it moved through the ice, dispatching sealers and picking up pelts, grinding the helpless babies beneath its bow. During those four hours, I counted forty-six pups slain by the ship. These will not be included in the quota, as only pelts brought aboard are counted.

Also, I witnessed thirteen pups being skinned alive.

In one case, a sealer happened to look my way, saw that he had my attention, and, grinning maliciously, he grabbed a pup by its flipper and turned him over on his back, and then slashed him open from neck to tail. He did not use the club at all.

8

Goodbye to Greenpeace

THINGS WERE COMING TO A BOIL between the leadership of Greenpeace and me when we returned to Vancouver. There was the usual fuss about paying off debts, and then I was hauled on the carpet by Pat Moore. I was, he felt, too much of an activist. He had told me that if he were elected president of Greenpeace, he would move to kick me out, and he was making good on that private campaign pledge.

But away from the foundation's internal politics, our work was having an impressive impact. I was astonished, for example, at the heart-warming turnout of students at the University of California in Berkeley to hear my report on the 1977 harp seal hunt. About seven hundred people gathered that April 7 on the steps of Sproul Hall, and, led by me and Gary Zimmerman, president of Greenpeace America, most marched to the Art Museum, where Prime Minister Pierre Trudeau was having lunch. Trudeau was visibly shaken when he emerged to a bilingual demonstration, with people chanting:

"Stop the slaughter!"

"Cessez le massacre!"

Support came, too, from the state legislature in Hawaii. The Hawaiian Senate applauded the resolution introduced by Rep. Leo J. Ryan (D-California) and passed by the U.S. House of Representatives, and another in the U.S. Senate by Sen. Spark M. Matsunaga (D-Hawaii) calling on Canada to "reassess its present policy of permitting the killing of newborn harp seals." The Hawaiian Senate, by its own resolution, gave full support to the Ryan-Matsunaga effort against what it called "the brutal and merciless slaughter of the seals."

And so it seemed to me that progress was being made, however slowly, and that this growing world concern was far more important than fighting over who sits above or below the salt in the Greenpeace hierarchy. What we were in danger of forgetting was why we undertook to protest the seal hunt in the first place. That decision was made primarily because, in addition to the possibility of saving seals, we could also call attention to the plight of all sea mammals. We saw the seals as a symbol through which we could dramatize the depletion and wholesale mismanagement of entire marine ecosystems. Ironically, the major result of our two anti-sealing expeditions was that the Canadian government, which more or less ignored Newfoundland as a rule, was now directing federal grants and programs toward the chronically poor people of that rocky outcropping in the Labrador Sea—and the slaughter of the harp seals went on.

In any event, the people in Vancouver who were running the Greenpeace Foundation decided I was one founder of the organization they could do without. Apparently, the ultimate transgression was that I had picked up a sealer's club and had thrown it into the water. I was voted out of Greenpeace. I vowed not to be bitter, and not even to look back, but to keep on going as my conscience dictated, to continue to be nonviolent and yet to defy authority whenever I considered it wrong—and whenever its policies worked against the sea mammals.

"You have no right to make yourself judge and jury," the Greenpeacers had told me, as I stood before them. "You have no right to appoint yourself a one-man vigilante squad."

That struck me as both extreme and unfair. But the attention of the organization seemed directed more now at working out little boxes and charts and creating an international complex of Greenpeacers that would be controlled out of a super-headquarters in Vancouver. Thus, it appeared, Greenpeace would spend so much of its time organizing and fund-raising that its efforts to conserve our planet would be dissipated. A million dollars in newly raised funds would not make a man or a woman face up to clubs and harpoons. That takes heart. And, as for the judge-and-jury charge, I told the Greenpeace board of directors something to this effect:

"Informed judgment of reasonable and humane people is the jury, and that verdict has been in for a long time. What is lacking is a police force to make the verdict stick.

"I guess I plead guilty to being a vigilante, but I can tell you something. If there are no police, then vigilantes will appear, because there will always be somebody to see to it that crime is never given a free rein."

It was an emotional parting. All of us had given too much of ourselves over too many years for there to be dispassionate goodbyes. Those in control at Greenpeace were going one way, others of us were going another. Soon after I was sacked, David Garrick sent in his resignation—not as a result of my departure, but because he was protesting creation of an international board to oversee policy and funding of all Greenpeace campaigns.

"This is the last straw," Garrick said. Like me, he cared little for form and everything for substance. No man had a better friend or stauncher ally than David Garrick, and I was gratified, though hardly surprised, to see him turn away from the direction in which Greenpeace was headed.

Severing my Greenpeace connections, as painful as it was, in no way diminished my activity. In fact, I felt more at liberty to pursue my own goals. The complications arising from Greenpeace's success were those I felt I should avoid at all cost. Thoreau had said, "Simplify, simplify, simplify," and I agreed with that. Some years earlier, I had put down three fundamental laws of ecology, and I reviewed them now as benchmarks in the struggle.

1. All forms of life are interdependent. The prey is as dependent upon the predator for control of its population as the predator is upon the prey for supply of food. Many people feel that eliminating mosquitoes is necessary for humans, but what of the swallows feeding on them? Do we want to do away with the swallows, too?

2. Diversity promotes stability. An ecosystem with hundreds of different species is far less likely to decline and disappear than one that has only a handful. The complex rain forest is more stable than the sparse Arctic tundra.

3. All resources are finite. As mankind uses the things of the earth, sometimes seemingly endless in our closed system, it is easy to lose sight of the immutable truth that everything has an end. Examples are almost too numerous and familiar to dwell upon—such as our energy and fuel shortage, and, of course, our ever-growing lists of endangered species.

There are other such laws, of course, and we ignore them all at our peril. Short-term economics must be made to give way to these rules of conservation and preservation. We must learn to live in harmony, not only with our fellow man, but with all the wonderful creatures of our planet.

This is really not as difficult a job as we tend to make it out to be. It is far too much to expect one person, or even a small group, to take on the job of assuring continued existence for all that is endangered in our world. But some good can be done, even by a small band, if it is made up of determined individuals—call them vigilantes, even—who devote their lives to the issue of survival, as I have devoted my life to saving whales and other sea mammals.

Those of us who do this kind of work are treated at times like escapees from a sideshow—weirdos who care more for animals than for humans. We are seen as vigilantes and radicals, revolutionaries and nonconformists, who, figuratively if not literally, are at peace with ourselves only when causing conflict.

I do not feel like a freak. I feel normal. And sometimes I wonder if the rest of the world is normal, especially that part of it that goes around plundering the natural world. It is at such times that the opposing philosophies of violence and nonviolence tear at me. I know violence is morally wrong and nonviolence is morally right. But what about results? Nonviolent action alone has seldom produced beneficial change on our planet. I continue to fret over this point. I compromise by allowing myself violence against property but never against life, human or otherwise.

After the blowup with Greenpeace, I moved my base of operations to Honolulu, Hawaii, where I lived for the rest of 1977 and most of 1978. Starlet Lum joined me there, and we led a very pleasant existence while I stepped up my writing in the field of active protectionism of mammals. I undertook to be, among other things, field correspondent for *Defenders of Wildlife* magazine in Washington, D.C. I also began doing more public speaking, and I never passed up an opportunity to address an audience, whether composed of experts or lay people.

On one speaking assignment, at a St. Louis, Missouri, Endangered Species Symposium hosted by Dr. Marlin Perkins, well-known for his "Wild Kingdom" television show about animals, I began to put together a new conservation organization. That was in June of 1977, and a group of us, including some old friends and some new ones, hoped to create an ecological activist power that might serve as the model for our times. We called it Earthforce, and we established headquarters in Vancouver.

Our philosophy was, if (as we knew to be true) one person, acting alone, could be heard, then a chorus of us might be able to gain even more attention with measurable results—if we did not get bogged down in details of organization. We meant to be activists in the strongest sense of the word. We expected that, by banding together, we as individuals could investigate crucial environmental problems, advise authorities in responsible positions, encourage some actions and oppose others, and in that way affect decisions about the basic environmental issues. From the start, we intended to be international in scope. We sought to bring about international commitments to preserve the habitats of wild animals and to foster deeper public understanding of the delicate interrelationship that binds all life together. We believed with the novelist Richard Adams that "each life is precious unto itself from the tiniest insect to the greatest tree," and with the late Justice William O. Douglas that man could "walk and live with humility and reverence . . . only when there is a wilderness. . . ."

Charter members of Earthforce included Al Johnson; Bruce Bunting, the Detroit veterinarian who had been with us on the ice; Bruce's father, Dr. A. L. Bunting, also from Detroit; and Ron Precious, whose documentary films on our forays had won prizes. These and others who joined Earthforce felt, along with me, that we were at a critical point in the survival expectations of a number of species, notably harp seals and many kinds of whales, as we had already dramatically demonstrated. We were convinced that Nature could overcome the damage already done, if ways to restrain the ravages of man could be found and enforced. We had to get back to a reasonable degree of ecological stability.

This meant direct action. We wanted to observe and demonstrate and testify and, backed by the force of facts and arguments, produce salutory changes. Earthforce was a society of direct actionists.

One of our other charter members was Cherry Clarke, who lived in Surrey, England, but had been born in Kenya. She agreed to work with us as a guide on Earthforce's first project, an expedition to East Africa to dramatize the current state of the elephant.

On New Year's Day of 1978, we flew to East Africa.

9

The Elephants

WE SWOOPED DOWN OVER the low-lying hills surrounding
Nairobi and landed at the Kenyan capital's little airport,
which, as I had been informed by my colleagues, was
extremely busy, if somewhat disorganized. The duty-
free shops were doing a brisk business. They were sell-
ing cut-rate liquor and other goods not only to depart-
ing tourists, which is what all countries do, but also to
those just arriving, which was extraordinary.

President Jomo Kenyatta of Kenya had decreed that
in less than three months the animal curio shops of Nairobi—which had the dubious distinction of being considered "the best in Africa"—would have to start
shutting down. As it turned out, this order was later
rescinded. But we had no way of knowing then that that
would happen, and one reason for our trip was to
gather photographic and other evidence of the size and
scope of the trade in animal products such as skins and
ivory, in advance of the closing of these stores.

Cliff Ward, a conservation activist who had lived in
East Africa for many years, had agreed to serve as our
man in that area. Ward was a native of White Cliff,
Michigan, and had made several walking tours of the
area, undertaking a trek of 1,200 miles on foot. Cliff
had made reservations for us at a small, out-of-the-way

hotel in Nairobi and had even arranged to have a rented van waiting for us.

Cherry Clarke, who was a friend of Bruce Bunting, had joined us in London, where we had stopped on our way over. She piled into a taxicab at the airport with the rest of us—Bruce Bunting and his father, Dr. Albert Bunting, plus Al Johnson and myself. It took about twenty minutes to make the ride into town. About halfway there, we passed the Nairobi National Park, which, I was told, contained some of all species of local animals except elephants, which struck me as a curious omission.

At the hotel, with Cherry staying behind, we loaded some photographic equipment aboard the van and drove to the main street, Kenyatta Avenue. Our first stop was the biggest shop we could find, called "Jewels and Antiquities," specializing in touristy souvenirs fashioned from the parts of African wildlife. Al, John, and Dr. Bunting waited in the back of the van while Bruce and I entered the store. All around were zebra-skin telephone book covers, lion's-paw desk lamps with shades made from ostrich eggs, baby-elephant-foot ashtrays, throw rugs created from the skins of colobus monkeys, an endangered species, and much more.

"How's business?" I asked a clerk who stood behind a small cash register near two enormous elephant tusks that gave the appearance of growing out of the floor.

"Quite good, thank you. May I help you?"

"Now that President Kenyatta has ordered all Kenyan curio shops closed by March twelfth, what will you do with all this stock? That's only about two and a half months away."

I said it quietly. But I may as well have shouted. The smile that had just begun to form on his face suddenly faded. His voice changed from all-out friendly to what the British call "correct."

"Oh, no problem. We will ship it to Hong Kong."

"But the law bans exports," I persisted. And that was as if I had slapped him.

"Who the hell are you? A journalist making trouble? I have nothing more to say to you!"

He turned away, and I went over to Bruce, who was setting up floodlights so that he could make some still photographs and run some film footage of the interior of the shop. But that was not to be.

I sensed it first, felt it rather than saw it—men advancing on us grimly from every quarter of the store. They seemed to be clerks and stock men from the back rooms, along with others who looked like salesmen and perhaps even warehousemen. I told Bruce it was time to go, and we made it through the front door and onto the street just a few feet ahead of the advance guard.

The first man through the door tripped and took a headlong spill onto the hard sidewalk. The shop manager, just behind him, delivered a swift kick to the rear of a guard at the door, apparently angered because he had let us out. Looking surprised, the guard dropped his billy club and fell down. The manager picked up the club, cursed, and flung it at him.

By that time, our pursuers had caught up with Bruce and me. One grabbed me by the arm and reached for my camera. Another jumped Bruce and still another punched at Bruce's camera. We shook them all loose and sprinted for the van. Bruce threw himself behind the wheel. I raced to the other side and flopped in.

Bruce got the engine started just as our pursuers arrived. He backed up with a jerk, shifted and shrieked away, leaving deep tire marks in the street. Close behind us came a blue sedan full of the men from the store, yelling and gesticulating.

"Hang on!" Bruce yelled, whipping around a corner, scattering pedestrians before him. "Hang on!"

I realized he was talking, not so much to me, as to his father and Al Johnson. We had left them comfortably relaxed in the back of the van. Our departure had been so sudden that we had not been able to tell them what was going on. It was too late now.

The blue sedan caught us. With a jarring crash, it plowed into the back of our van. And then it was alongside us, crunching into the driver's door with its front fender as we sped along the street, narrowly missing dozens of terrified pedestrians. We sailed up onto the sidewalk and came to a halt.

The men were all around us, pounding on the windows and trying to force open the locked doors. They demanded our film. We tossed out a couple of unexposed cartridges, but our pursuers did not fall for that old ruse. They yelled and beat on the van and continued to demand our film when, to our blessed relief, we heard the sound of a police siren.

However, the police had no interest in our side of the story. We were all arrested and marched back to the store. The police inspector in charge ordered us to keep quiet while the store manager gave an impassioned account of how we came into his store and asked disputatious questions. It was a true, if heavily biased, account. When he finished, I started to give my side. The inspector cut me short.

"Mr. Shah here is a taxpayer. You, my friends, are not. You have nothing to say."

He then explained that we were guilty of being unauthorized and unregistered journalists.

"But we are not journalists," I said. "We are conservationists interested in the survival of wildlife in Kenya."

He thought a moment. Then he announced that he was changing the charge. It would be impersonation of journalists.

Our cameras were seized and we were ordered into our van, with a constable along to give us directions to the police station. The inspector and three other officers rode in the police car following closely behind. The policeman's directions took us, not to jail, but to a winding, seedy alley that came to a deadend against a big stone wall. Al Johnson was ordered out of the van to the police car.

"We do not wish to inconvenience you," the inspector told him. "If you can make us happy, perhaps we can make you happy."

Happiness in Nairobi that day was the equivalent of ninety American dollars. We paid, got our cameras back, bade the police a polite goodbye, and drove out of the *cul de sac*.

With Cliff Ward's guidance, we had staked out Kenya, Uganda, Sudan, Tanzania, and Zambia for our photography, cinematography, and interviews. We had sent out questionnaires weeks earlier to a list of wildlife experts in Africa that Cliff had compiled. What we hoped to do was put together a picture of the systematic decimation of the African elephant. The data we collected would be passed on to Rep. Anthony C. Beilenson (D-California), who had been working for years to get the African elephant placed on the U.S. endangered-species list or, failing that, to ban or curtail African ivory imports into the United States.

The arithmetic is against the elephants. Slain by poachers by the tens of thousands every year, their bodies are left to rot and to be picked over by hyenas and vultures. Their ivory tusks are sawed away from their bloody carcasses, to be shipped by the ton to warehouses or to dim back rooms where workmen with jewelers' saws carve out beads and other *objets d'art.* The traffic is so spirited that the same quality of elephant ivory that brought thirty cents per pound in the 1950s is going now for thirty dollars per pound—an increase of one thousand percent. And it is going up as the number of elephants declines and nations like the United States contemplate protecting them against extinction. The scarcity of ivory real and threatened, drives up the price, and makes the traffic—legal and illegal—all the more attractive, especially to those who would like to get rich quickly.

The issue was a good first test for our new organization. I became convinced of this after reading Iain and Oria Douglas-Hamilton's book *Among the Elephants,* which laid out the problem graphically. Greenpeace and the other groups with which I was familiar had not involved themselves directly with the elephant as an endangered species, and there was no sustained follow-up to help avert the grim future seen by the Douglas-Hamiltons.

This dedicated couple was in the midst of a new study in 1978. Their survey aimed to determine precisely how many African elephants were surviving the encroachment of farms and ranchlands on their feeding grounds, the hunting for hides and meat and tusks, and now—with increased protection of elephants in game preserves and national parks—the rise of large-scale poaching.

The Douglas-Hamilton survey, begun in 1976, was completed in 1979. It covered thirty-five countries and was sponsored by the World Wildlife Fund, the New York Zoological Society, and the International Union for Conservation of Nature. It consisted primarily of an aerial census, doublechecked on the ground, and it produced alarming statistics. These showed that the African elephant population, once thought to be "millions and millions," actually totaled little more than 1.3 million. They were being killed faster than they could reproduce.

In March of 1976, at the outset of their census-taking, the Douglas-Hamiltons found seventy-eight carcasses and fifty-eight live elephants in fifteen minutes at Uganda's Ruwenzori National Park. Later, at Kabalega Falls Park in Uganda, they counted nine hundred elephants lying dead, purportedly cut down by automatic weapons fired by close associates of Idi Amin, who was then president. When Amin was overthrown in 1979, many such weapons fell into the hands of poachers, making them too great a match for outgunned game wardens. By 1981, the elephant population of Uganda had been virtually wiped out.

According to the Douglas-Hamiltons, Nairobi used to be the center of ivory smuggling from Uganda, Zaire, and Tanzania; more than four hundred tons were exported in 1976. But the traffic has been curtailed, they said, and even in Kenya's Tsavo National Park "one rarely sees a dead elephant."

Since completing the elephant census, Oria Douglas-Hamilton has had some second thoughts about her earlier count of 1.3 million. In a 1980 report, she suggested that that total might have been a "great overestimate, considering the amount of ivory still flowing out of the continent." Even so, efforts to clamp down on the ivory trade, such as the Convention on International Trade in Endangered Species, clearly are not achieving complete success.

"There is money to be made in ivory," one dealer in Yaoundé, the capital of Cameroon, told Oria Douglas-Hamilton. He said he had ten carvers, each able to finish a statuette or figurine worth one hundred American dollars every day. And he added: "Plenty of orders. I have a special order from France to produce ivory porno all year round."

Both the African elephant (*Loxodonta africana*) and the Asiatic elephant (*Elephas maximus*), the last survivors of the mammalian order *Proboscidea,* are descended from a pig-sized creature (*Palaemastodon*) that has been extinct for some thirty million years. The Asiatic elephant has long been used for transport and as a work animal in India, Burma, Thailand, and elsewhere. The African elephant, slightly larger (ten or eleven feet high at full growth), usually runs wild. His tusks are bigger and finer. His meat on sale in an African market goes for fifty-five cents per pound, and his hide brings $1,200 to be cut up for briefcases, handbags, wallets, and shoes. His feet become wastepaper baskets, umbrella stands, and the like, and his fat is melted down for cooking oil.

I do not agree with the Douglas-Hamiltons that it is necessary at times to cull the herds, in order to make way for man's expansion into elephant country. I believe we should limit man in taking away the elephants' territory, not curb the number of elephants to fit the territory we are willing to begrudge them. I do agree with Oria Douglas-Hamilton's sentiments, however, when she comments, as she did in her 1980 report:

"To see the elephants shot in masses, especially a whole family, is a most horrific experience. It is easy for armchair ecologists to recommend shooting programs when they have never participated in the shooting. But hearing the guns mixed with the screams and bellowing of the terrified elephants as they all collapse needs a strong stomach and a cold nerve."

We were glad to get out of Nairobi, with its tall buildings and bustling traffic, to make our "see for yourself" visit to Kenya's game preserves. We took on fresh supplies and secured a new vehicle—a land cruiser. We traveled south out of Nairobi on the Mombasa highway in high spirits. Within a few hours, we ran out of asphalt and were on dusty gravel, but eager to reach the Tsavo National Park. We had a rare treat. On our drive into the park just before sunset, the lush greenness was breath-taking. Several zebras ran along with us as we wound our way up a hill. Suddenly, at the crest, we saw a big waterhole, surrounded by about forty elephants drinking and spraying themselves, some with the red dust of Tsavo, others with water.

The matriarch held her position of leadership at the head of the herd. Massive and proud, she stood swaying in the evening air, looking about warily, protectively. Behind her, the herd plodded about with heavy grace, muddying the water with massive, clay-smeared bodies, sending giant ripples across to the opposite bank, where skittish storks broke and ran at the slightest hint of trouble.

There was no sign on the main road of poachers, although we had heard that about 1,300 of them were operating in the park. Later, at Ambsaseli, we saw the evidence—bones strewn about, and the skulls of elephants with their tusks sawed off. It was not on the main road, where the tourists came, but in the bush, where the poachers were, that the elephants died.

At the foot of Mount Kenya, we were with Warden Peter Jenkins when he received an urgent radio call. He rushed away, and we followed. Two of his rangers had been ambushed by poachers about three miles away, he told us. One man was dead, and the other seriously wounded.

On the scene, we found several park rangers bending over their bleeding comrade. A few feet away, the figure of another ranger lay sprawled in an awkward, unmoving pile of dusty, bloody uniform. His head had been blown open, apparently by a bullet.

When the injured man and his dead partner were taken away, Warden Jenkins went over the ground. He found some spent cartridges and examined them carefully. He showed us some markings and identified the shell casings as government military issue. It was not a particularly strong clue, he said. The ammunition could have been stolen, almost anywhere, at any time.

We thought we had come upon a great story, but Jenkins shrugged aside the idea. He said that such murders are seldom treated as news in Nairobi. Incidents like these were quite common. The poachers were Somalis, he said, and they were mean and tough. Only a few months earlier, he recalled, Warden Ken Clark of Galan Game Ranch had been shot and killed instantly. Seven Somali tribesmen were hunted down by military personnel and killed in a shootout.

Jenkins' men found a campsite, apparently used by the killers. There were a few small tusks, a couple of skins, many bones, and some dried, smoked meat. The two rangers might have seen the smoke or simply stumbled accidentally into the camp, Jenkins said, and were shot as they looked it over.

Two days later, back in Nairobi, Bruce Bunting and I discussed the killing with a tall, powerfully built black

Kenyan named Mennasses Otto Keiller, who had a reputation as an incorruptible, tireless fighter against poaching. He was pointed out to us as the standard bearer of the conservationists' struggle to save the elephant through government actions.

Keiller told us he had been shot at many times—in the bush and even on the streets of Nairobi. He said the poachers had put a price on his head. And he added:

"These men will do almost anything to see me dead. I'm bad for profits.

"It is most ironic. While I must struggle to obtain one workable Land Rover because my government budget cannot afford it, the poachers have enough money to purchase a dozen easily. The poachers are able to trace our movements. They simply stop operating while we are in their area. If they are arrested, their family is protected and provided for by the secret criminals supporting them. The poachers have wealthy sponsors. The local man in the bush has five advocates when we get him into court. There is, you see, a Kenyan Mafia.

"But you, the people overseas, can hurt their profits more than I can. I can only stop the expendable ones in the bush. I can't reach the big fish. You can. If you didn't buy the stuff, there would be no work for poachers."

It was a complex web that we found in Kenya—illegal ivory warehouses, allegations of bribes to keep journalists from probing too closely into the ivory and curio trade, poachers who are better armed, better informed, more efficient, and better paid than the wardens and rangers, who are consistently frustrated and intimidated by the very criminals they are supposed to contain.

Oddly enough, the Kenyans who care are looking outward, not inward, for solutions. They point out that Americans purchase 24 percent of the annual elephant harvest—most of which is illegal—and they applaud any actions that would internationalize the problem. The theory is that when the current market dries up, the illegal taking of the animals will cease.

Our studies were turned over to the U.S. Office of Endangered Species and to committees of the U.S. Congress that deal with the subject. Earthforce brought the greatest pressure there because a U.S. ban against the import of African ivory would mark the greatest contribution yet to the defense of this great animal. In 1976 alone, the volume of ivory purchased by Americans required the deaths of 13,218 elephants.

In their search for more and more ivory, importers complain that tusks are getting smaller. The reason? Hunters over the years have singled out the best bulls with the largest tusks. Thus the genetically superior bulls are removed from the herds, and smaller tusks are bred.

With scarcities come substitutions. In one San Francisco shop, I saw an entire uncarved tusk in the window for $15,000, and on a shelf inside there was an intricately carved whole tusk also priced at $15,000. In another store, I inquired about a tusk that was fully carved but that did not look exactly right. The shopkeeper confessed that it was a fake.

It was whalebone, shaped and carved to look like ivory.

10

The Sea Shepherd

AS A NEW ORGANIZATION, Earthforce had frustrations in abundance. We knew what had to be done. We knew how to do it. We had all the necessary capabilities for an effective conservation effort—all, that is, except one: money. Not enough people had heard of us for any direct-mail fund-raising drive, or any other method of raising capital that we had used at Greenpeace. We had collected our first-hand data on elephants and turned that over to interested members of the U.S. Congress. We had put together filmed and photographed evidence of the illegal slaughtering of African elephants, and presented that, too, to responsible authorities. But we had done all of that with our own money. And now there was no more.

We felt stymied, particularly as the Canadian harp seal hunt would be starting again in mid-March of 1979, just a few months off, and we were receiving continuing reports on illegal whaling operations. It was maddening to have everything coming together but the wherewithal—solid intelligence reports, the know-how, the experience, the will, but no money.

One idea that presented itself was to get in touch with other organizations and propose that, in exchange for financing, I would lead an expedition against the sealers in March and a later one against the whalers as a representative of the contributing groups. I offered to do all the work, organize and conduct the sorties, and carry the organizations' banners into the confrontations. I sent off the proposals and waited.

The only response came from Cleveland Amory of the Fund for Animals in New York City. The Fund's Washington, D.C., office had been leading the fight to get the African elephant listed as endangered and protected from demands of the United States market. Amory said he was interested and would like to meet with me. We arranged to meet at the Beverly Hills Hotel.

I flew from Hawaii, where Starlet Lum and I were then living, to Los Angeles, and jumped into a taxicab at the airport. I had no idea then of the great distances that people travel in that area, and the long ride and twenty-dollar fare to Beverly Hills were a shock.

As at our first meeting in St. Louis, the size and commanding presence of Cleveland Amory were intimidating. I am not a small man, but around "the Bear," I sometimes get the feeling that I am. It never is anything he does consciously, for his manner is always impeccably cordial. That morning, he sought to put me at ease by offering breakfast, but I declined, and he went straight to the point.

"What can you do?" he asked.

"Well," I said, "we can go out on the ice off Newfoundland and upset the seal hunt. We can spray organic dye that's harmless to the seals but destroys the economic value of the pelts, and frustrate them that way."

"How would you get in there?"

"Either of two ways," I said. "The low-cost way, for

about twenty-five thousand dollars, is to fly a crew in and drop them out on the ice by parachute. It's extremely dangerous, but we can do it. We can get out there and we can do it."

I had never done any parachuting, but I had thought about this method of surprising the sealers for a long time. With the new parachutes that let jumpers down to soft landings and that could even be steered and made to hover, we should be able to pull off such an operation. I contemplated a minimum of training. Yet, it could be dangerous because of the panning of the ice and the great gaps that often appeared between floes. A parachutist who landed in the water between the pans, or whose weight tilted a small pan so that he was dumped into the water, might come up under the ice and be drowned before he could be helped or fight his way to safety on the surface.

Amory looked as if he might have thought of all that, too.

"Is there anything that's less dangerous?" he asked.

"Yes. The other way to do it—it's safer, but more expensive—is to take a ship in."

"Do you know where to get a ship?"

"Well, I have an idea where I could find one, whether I charter one or buy one. I think it would be cheaper to buy than charter. Charter prices would run about one hundred thousand dollars for two months."

"Okay," he said. "We'll take it from there."

A few days later I met Amory again in New York City. He gave me $1,000 to go look for a ship. He wanted to give me more, but I insisted that was all I needed for expenses for the time being. I flew to London by Laker Airlines for $135. From London, I went by train to Athens and flew from there to the island of

Rhodes, where a friend, David Sellers, showed me available fishing boats. I wanted a fishing boat because they are such sturdy, economical craft. They are built to operate in the roughest of seas, and, because the margin of profit is rather close in the fishing business, their engines are miserly in fuel consumption. David and I found nothing we liked in Rhodes or in Greece, where we also looked, and we moved on to Holland, where we knew there were solidly built fishing vessels. Nothing turned up there, and I returned to London.

In London, I learned from friends in the business that ships were being sold in Grimsby. I found one there, but, after having a preliminary survey made of her, decided not to take her. I moved on to Hull, where, to my surprise, there was a veritable grab bag of fishing boats, veterans of the "cod wars" off Iceland, laid up idle and available for purchase.

Of all those I looked at, the *Westella* was the most appealing, for practical reasons, such as her solid construction—at a highly respected shipyard at Beverly-on-Humber—her record at sea, and for reasons having nothing to do with practicality: She had been launched on March 15, 1960; Starlet, with whom I discussed the whole situation by long-distance telephone, liked the date because March 15 was her birthday, and I liked it because it was the traditional starting date of the Newfoundland hunt for baby harp seals that I hoped to use the craft to end.

The *Westella* was 206 feet long and weighed 779 tons—a Yorkshire deep-water trawler designed for a life of hard work in the frigid and stormy seas of the North Atlantic from Scotland to the Arctic Circle. She had served her masters well. Three times she won the Silver Cod Trophy, a prize highly coveted by the tough fishermen of the area and so well regarded officially that the Queen's husband, the Duke of Edinburgh, went aboard her to make the award. Speed, capacity, economy, efficiency—these were some of the qualities the British looked for in making the award, and they were what we wanted, too.

The *Westella* had fished mostly in the White Sea, Barent's Sea, and the North Sea. In all of her nineteen rugged years, only once had she had a scuffle—with a Soviet destroyer in the White Sea, a little sideswiping. When Britain ended its "cod war" with Iceland by agreeing to cut back severely on its cod fleet, she was laid up with seventy or eighty like her at St. Andrew's dock in Kingston-on-Hull. There was no place else to go. She would cost $2 million to replace, but I picked her up for $120,000.

Until her last fishing run in August 1978, the *Westella* had been run by J. Marr and Son, of Hull. The Marr family was related by marriage to a family that owned and operated a fruit plantation somewhere, and the Marr vessels, perhaps for that reason, were painted yellow and referred to locally as "the banana boats." The years had not been too kind to the paint, or maybe the yellow had always looked bad. In any case it was certainly a ghastly color. With rust showing through the bilious ochre, or whatever it was, the *Westella,* when I first saw her, looked like a scabrous, dying thing. But there is rust and there is rust. Underneath, when I had her blasted, was pure, unpitted metal.

I decided to do a thorough checkup and I had her hauled out of the water for stem-to-stern, keel-to-mast scrutiny. That cost about $4,000, but it was worth it. Cleveland Amory, true to his promise, managed to scrape together $120,000 in New York and send it to me. We completed the sale on December 5, 1978.

In the survey, handled by our broker, Nigel Burgess, Ltd., of London, the *Westella* proved to be very strong in fitness tests, ultra-sonic vibrations applied and evaluated by Duff and Company. Chipping, blasting, wirebrushing, paint—all such cosmetic ministrations that would prepare the ship for her visual impact on the world did not especially concern me, for those tasks were well within our abilities to perform. What I wanted to make sure of—even at the cost of a precious $4,000— was that she was seaworthy, economical, and tough enough to do the difficult job ahead. And she was.

On December 15, 1978, she was rechristened the *Sea Shepherd*. The name was my idea and I insisted on it as the most appropriate one we could think of. Starlet and I had spent much time discussing and arguing over names when we were not bogged down in the interminable paperwork involved in the process of acquiring the ship. Starlet was invaluable at every stage, and it was evident that we were growing into a close-knit team. Mark Sterk joined us from America and immediately put his artistic skill to work. With the ship now registered to me as owner and operator, and certified as ready to sail (officially Lloyd's 100 A-1), Sterk painted on her new name in white.

More good news followed. We had appealed to the prestigious British Royal Society for the Prevention of Cruelty to Animals, for financial help. Now, the society came through with a grant of about $48,000. This fresh money arrived December 20, and with it I paid for the survey, fuel, supplies, and the hiring of a crew to deliver the ship to Boston, where we intended to prepare secretly for our run through the ice to Newfoundland and the Labrador Front. We also bought a second-hand Loran C long-range radar—a prize piece of navigational gear for us.

I hired a captain and a mate, a radio operator who was also a mate, three engineers, and a deckhand. We filled out the crew with our volunteers—Starlet and me, Joe Goodwin and Erin McMullin (she had come with him from San Diego, California, while we were readying the trawler), Mark Sterk, also from San Diego, and Richard Jordan, son of Bill Jordan, wildlife director of the Royal Society.

We left Hull on a cold and blustery January 3, 1979. To save about $800 in pilots' fees I decided not to go around the south of England through the English Channel. Instead, we went around Scotland, and that was fine, for a terrible storm struck the south and destroyed four fishing boats. A storm hit Scotland the day after we passed, and Ireland the day following our passage there. We felt lucky and vaguely guilty, as if we were a Typhoid Mary of the sea, being around but never suffering catastrophe—just as that old lady had spread typhoid wherever she went in nineteenth century New York City but never fell sick herself.

The *Sea Shepherd* handled smoothly, and she proved very economical, burning only four tons of fuel per day. Her total fuel capacity was two hundred tons. Fully running, at four tons per day, that gave her quite a few days at sea, and she had a range between twelve thousand and fourteen thousand miles, depending upon how hard she was pushed.

From the Azores all the way to Boston, we had warm, clear weather. We were comfortable wearing T-shirts south of Newfoundland. It was not until about fifty miles out of Boston that we began to feel the cold. Leslie Fewster, our first mate and veteran of many voyages in the North Atlantic, called our trip "the miracle crossing."

Be that as it may, the miracle for me was running along for about an hour with six blue whales. The biggest was half as long as the *Sea Shepherd*—about 60 feet, which seemed immense to me, although I knew blue whales fully grown ran up to 90 feet, and the largest ever killed was 118 feet long.

We had hoped to keep our arrival in Boston a secret. But some of our friends ashore had other ideas, and there was a story in the Boston *Globe* all about our aims and missions, and more specifically our intention to push through the ice floes and get out to the sealers by the middle of March. It probably made little difference to our security. After our two brushes with the Seal Protection Act, in 1976 and 1977, it was logical to assume that the Canadian government was keeping close tabs on our movements.

We sailed into Boston January 15, 1979, and, even though the crossing had been idyllic, we were all pretty happy to see it end. The seven rough-hewn Yorkshire fishermen who were making the trip for pay were basically at odds with the six younger volunteers, mostly landlubbers with predilections—like vegetarianism, conservation of natural resources, and animal welfare—annoying to the other seven. Also, having two women aboard did not go down well with the professionals.

There were conflicts and arguments, usually of the senseless, bickering variety that went nowhere, over the morality of killing whales and seals versus the necessity of man's survival in a fundamentally hostile world. First Mate Leslie Fewster and Engineer Stan Johnson sided with our argument that man was taxing the sea and that it was a good idea for people like us to make a dramatic, if dangerous, defense of sea mammals. On the other hand, Captain Jeff Twidle and Chief Engineer Leslie

Smith were appalled that an honest fishing trawler out of their native Yorkshire would be used to thwart those who made their living off the sea's inhabitants, and they regarded Fewster and Johnson as traitors to their class.

And so I sighed with relief as we sighted the lights of Boston. The conflicts had made it a long thirteen days. We entered the harbor and dropped anchor at the foot of one of the runways at Logan Airport. Almost immediately, a new set of troubles arose—bureaucratic harassment, derisive treatment by the news media, and even what could only be called sabotage.

Boston is a proud city, rich in the heritage of the American spirit to which it has contributed so heavily. This, to me, was almost palpable as we edged gently into our berthing. I had a sudden flash of what this harbor must have been like in 1773, full of tea and Yankee indignation against the British crown. How like those protestors I felt! And, with my bent to the sea, I was one, also, with the men of the magnificent clipper ships, like the *Flying Cloud,* built here in the mid-1800s. The Massachusetts Port Authority (Massport) greeted us with the news that we were welcome only if we paid $100 per day. For a noncommercial vessel, that sounded enormous, especially since a big freighter in front of us was paying $100 per day. We had no choice, however, and our two-month stay, as we readied for our run at the sealers, cost us more than $6,000.

We had to undergo a thorough search by the U.S. Coast Guard before being allowed to tie up at the army dock. It seemed like undue attention, and hints were dropped that officials had been told we had illegal drugs aboard. We did not, as the search showed.

Soon after, as I prepared flight reservations to get our hired crew back to England, Joe Goodwin came by to report he had just seen Terry Grayson, our radio operator, put a small piece of machinery on the edge of the deck, about a quarter of an inch from falling over. Goodwin said he was puzzled, especially as he had the feeling he had surprised Grayson in the act of throwing the thing over the side.

I went with him to investigate. Just as he had said, we found a small piece of machinery, about a foot long, well-oiled, with two brass bearings on the end.

"What is it, Paul?" Goodwin asked.

I had no idea. I asked him to take it to Grayson for an explanation. Then I began to remember a few things about Grayson, who had aroused our suspicions considerably on the trip over. He had come on board as a friend of Captain Jeff Twidle. It had been a long time since he had sailed as a radio operator, but he had a wide variety of other credentials—he was a deep-sea diver and a demolitions expert, and had been ticketed in Sperry gyro gear. He shook me up at one point, when we were not even talking about the seals, by suddenly blurting, "You know, I could finish off one of those sealing vessels with cordite explosives around it that could blow the props off, and I could do it for ten thousand dollars a day."

I mumbled something like, "Well, I don't know anything about that," and changed the subject. My suspicions were intensified.

Grayson spent a lot of time sending and receiving messages in Morse code, but, when I asked whom he was talking to, he replied, "Oh, nobody in particular. . . . Just getting back into practice." And, later, in Boston, when he met Cleveland Amory, he said, "You look older than your pictures." I wondered what pictures he had seen. How had a Yorkshire fisherman learned about sealing ships and seen pictures of Cleveland Amory in a village like Hull?

With the strange piece of machinery in my hand, and Grayson's background in gyroscopic equipment on my mind, I descended to the steering-gear room and looked around. I noticed two pegs that were holding nothing. I fitted the piece onto the pegs. It lined up perfectly and dropped into place. The piece was the linkage for the automatic steering. Without it, we would have been disabled, unable to steer except laboriously by hand.

By that time, Grayson had locked himself up on the bridge with the captain. Young Richard Jordan went there to start his watch, but Captain Twidle and Grayson yelled at him to go away. I called the Boston police, who referred me to the Massachusetts state police, who told me to call the U.S. Coast Guard, which said I should get in touch with the Boston police—a perfect circle.

"Look," I said. "One of you should get over here instead of giving me the run-around."

They all came. Sixty policemen were running all over the place. Television crews, too.

"Hey, I just wanted a couple of guys over here to talk to these fellows," I said. But things were out of control. I must have dispensed five pounds of coffee that night. The Boston police, the Massachusetts state police, the Coast Guard, the Coast Guard intelligence—they were all there, and, a few minutes later, U.S. Army military police came running up the gangplank with guns drawn.

"Where's the mutiny?" they shouted. "Who's shot?"

Through it all, with one police car after another arriving to disgorge their contingents, each from a different arm of the law, and with me being interviewed and interrogated relentlessly in the captain's lounge,

Captain Twidle and his radio operator never left the bridge. Despite all the commotion, which must have resembled a remake of some Keystone Kops Komedy, the captain never once came out to ask what was going on.

The various police questioned everybody. Grayson showed no pleasure in being the star of the show. He twitched constantly and sweated profusely under interrogation.

"Do you want him locked up?" one of the policemen asked.

"No," I said, after consulting a couple of lawyers I had called, one, our friend Ed Walsh, from the Fund for Animals and the other a distinguished maritime lawyer named Tom Muzyka, who also held a mate's license. "No. Just get him out of here."

The next day, Captain Twidle appeared on deck with his personal gear and announced he was headed for the airport. I told him he could not remove anything from the ship until immigration authorities had given us clearance.

"I can do whatever I bloody well want," he said.

"Well, you might be captain at sea, but you're not in charge here, in port," I said. "I'm in charge here, I'm the owner of this vessel, and I say you just stay right here. I'm not going to pay any fine because you're jumping ship."

"I'm not jumping ship," he said. "I'm just taking my things to the airport."

With that, he left the ship. Grayson, who had been lurking in the background, went with him. On a hunch, I checked over the ship's stack of passports. The captain's and the radio operator's were missing. It was clear that they were, indeed, jumping ship.

"Oh, God," I said aloud. "Here we go again."

I called immigration and had Twidle and Grayson arrested at the airport. When they were brought back aboard, they complained bitterly. I insisted they could not have their passports until immigration authorities said so, and I stuck to that. It would have been an intolerable bureaucratic hassle to bring any charges, and so we just let them go back to England.

But before that, Tom Muzyka walked all over the ship with Captain Twidle and checked out all the equipment. Muzyka, with his first-mate's eye, spotted a number of things that were wrong—wires removed from the radio equipment, bolts loosened on the steering gear, and, of course, the automatic-steering linkage that had been removed and had not yet been firmly refastened—and pointed them out to the captain, who was taken aback by the lawyer's knowledge of ships. We had the captain sign a certification that the *Sea Shepherd* was mechanically sound and seaworthy.

Thanks to our television coverage in Boston and stories in Boston newspapers, whatever secrecy we had hoped for was long gone. As we put together a crew for the run up to Newfoundland's ice, and worked also on dealing with a myriad of requests from news people who wanted to go along, I was concerned that no last-minute trap should be sprung to delay our projected departure.

"Look, we're going to leave here on the first of March," I told the U.S. Coast Guard. "I don't want you coming down here on the last day of February to say I need a safety inspection or a fire inspection. Please, tell me now, and let's get it over with."

"Oh, no," the Coast Guard people said. "We're satisfied that everything's in order."

That was in January. We went ahead frantically to

ready our scheduled March 1 departure. On February 28, though, there was the U.S. Coast Guard, inspecting us!

"What the hell are you guys doing?" Tom Muzyka demanded.

"The Canadian Department of Transport asked us to do this," came the frank reply. We were of British registry, and we wondered what the Canadian connection was. The only thing we could figure was that it was a courtesy between coast guards, the Canadian Department of Transport being the parent for the Canadian Coast Guard, as the U.S. Department of Transportation now contains the U.S. Coast Guard.

"Where's your safety inspection certificate?" the U.S. Coast Guard asked.

We had to explain that the British do not require the fishing vessels they register to maintain safety records, nor do they issue safety inspection certificates. But the questions kept coming, and as the *Sea Shepherd* was inspected for this and inspected for that it became quite apparent that the object was delay. We had Tom Muzyka fly to Washington, D.C., and explain our situation to U.S. Coast Guard headquarters, which relayed the word to Boston to leave us alone.

Next came the British consul in Boston, with a flurry of inquiries and forms to fill out. When we had satisfied that interest, the U.S. Customs people came aboard to check us out. We explained that we had already had our papers checked. Why go over all that again? The American Customs officials said they were acting on a request from Canadian Immigration. Finally, on March 3—two days after we had planned to leave—the man from Lloyd's arrived to make a survey. We had to show that our ship had just passed its annual inspection and had even been up for a special inspection, good until 1981. But the Lloyd's inspector would not clear us for sea until we had strengthened some hull supports, all about ten feet above the water line, that he found too weak. The only welders I could get on short notice was a union crew from Bethlehem Steel, which worked all night and charged us $3,000 to replace the supports. Approving the work, the Lloyd's man found a bulkhead that he said had to be replaced. We could see he was out to nibble us to death, and we turned to our resourceful maritime lawyer once more.

"Look, do you want a lawsuit?" Muzyka asked the Lloyd's representative. "Just tell us what we have to get done and then shove off. You can't come in here and say, 'Get this done' and, 'Get that done,' and keep us hanging day to day. There isn't a ship in the world that is built well enough to pass a Coast Guard safety inspection if you don't want us to go to sea."

And so, finally, finally—we were allowed to leave the port of Boston, but under almost constant aerial surveillance on the high seas by Canadian Coast Guard planes as we sailed north. With the passage of time, there have been periods when I wondered if I had just imagined harassment. But the proof that it was real was that, when we returned to Boston after the harp seal hunt, and when we sailed again, but in the opposite direction, nobody came around to see our papers, to pore over clearances with meticulous attention, or to be concerned about the state of our vessel.

Dozens of volunteer plumbers, welders, carpenters, and painters from the Boston area had turned the ugly-duckling *Westella* into the sleek and handsome *Sea Shepherd* during our two months in port. We had sand-blasted her hull, varnished her woodwork, and given her a clean, bright look.

We also had loaded forty tons of rock ballast and reinforced her bow with eighteen tons of concrete poured into a ballast chamber. We wanted some authority down there when we pushed up against the heavy ice floes in the Gulf of St. Lawrence.

We took on some of the volunteer workers as crew members to be among the thirty-two persons aboard when we sailed. Eddy Smith, a painter, and Paul Pezwick, a plumber, joined us as oilers, for example. Keith Krueger came from Honolulu to be a deckhand, and my father, Tony Watson, came down from Canada to be our ship's cook.

As first mate, I had my friend, Matt Herron, a journalist, photographer, and sailor from Sausalito, California, who had sailed his own small boat from Florida to Africa and written a book about it. As second mate, I hired an Englishman named Tony Taylor, who was located in Maine by a yacht agency.

Representing the sponsoring Fund for Animals was our benefactor himself, Cleveland Amory, heading a team that included a Fund lawyer, photographer, press coordinator, two film-makers, and a Fund field agent from Texas. The Royal Society for Prevention of Cruelty to Animals sent along an RSPCA inspector from England.

Also, we still had Starlet, Joe Goodwin, and Mark Sterk, as well as radio operator David McKenney and three hired members of the crew that had made the transatlantic crossing aboard the *Sea Shepherd*—Leslie Fewster, Charles Ralph, and Leslie Smith. Fewster was now our captain.

There were also a dozen news people aboard. Technically, they were crew members, too, because the British consul had ordered as a condition of our maintaining our British license that we carry "no passengers." We lost a National Broadcasting Company television crew on that account. Rather huffily, the NBC people said their journalistic objectivity would be compromised if they signed on as crew members, however superficial and technical an act that might be. I told them I would be glad to fire them as soon as we reached international waters, but they would have none of that. The twelve who did go along included Sid Moody of the Associated Press and Sunny Lewis of Vancouver radio station CHUM/CFUN, who proved to be cheerful and useful helpers—Sid pitching in with the navigation and Sunny with radio communications. Others were Larry Manning of the Los Angeles *Herald Examiner* and Maggie Hall and Eric Piper of the London *Daily Mirror,* as well as Tom Bevier of the Detroit *Free Press* and Tom Schell of American Broadcasting Company.

And so, despite everything, we were finally pulled together. With our "crew" of thirty-two, a small crowd of well-wishers on the dock to see us off, and the chaplain of Boston Harbor, the Reverend Wally Cedarleaf, to give us a blessing, we cast off from the U.S. Army dock that had been our home for two months.

It was early on the morning of March 3, 1979. The day was cold and clear and our spirits were high. The sun came up and over us and the tall buildings of Boston shrank away to a blur off our fantail.

The *Sea Shepherd,* her engines humming like larks, headed for the open sea and the ice-bound Gulf of St. Lawrence to the north.

11

Shepherd *on the Ice*

As usual, not all of those aboard were ambulatory on the second day at sea. Some, notably among the reporters, lay moaning in their bunks. Others, with more spunk than seaworthiness, refused to surrender to *mal de mer* and walked about with the look and vitality of zombies. Sunny Lewis, for example, refused to miss any of her watches, even though she spoke little and had turned a delicate shade of green.

Mark Sterk and Paul Pezwick, also made of stern stuff, spent that day—Sunday, March 4, 1979—stowing helicopter jet fuel on deck, making sure it was properly lashed down. As for me, as owner of the vessel and leader of the expedition, I was kept busy from the very first day mediating disputes. With basically three worlds to coordinate—the conservationists, the professional sailors, and the news media—I rarely had a moment when one or another was not raging at something or somebody. I often thought Columbus was lucky: all he had to contend with were seamen who believed, as an article of faith, that the earth was flat.

One thing soon became apparent: no matter how much we paid the hired hands, they were never satisfied. The volunteers worked hard and long, rarely balking at tasks assigned to them. They were, therefore, to be preferred.

The next day, Monday, we cut our speed drastically. We had entered the Cabot Strait that leads into the Gulf of St. Lawrence—with Nova Scotia's Cape Breton Island to the west, off our portside, and the southwest tip of Newfoundland to the east, off our starboard. The ice pack was solid there. Without icebreaker sawteeth on our prow, we could not break up the four-foot-thick layer, and so we sawed and chopped our way through. The noise sounded like something out of the Devil's machine shop, a screaming and a grating that set our teeth on edge and raised the hair on the back of our necks. If Roméo LeBlanc, Canada's Minister of Fisheries, could have heard it he would have been pleased. He had predicted in parliamentary debates that we could not possibly make it through the thick ice. But we kept plowing ahead. We would haul back and go full speed ahead until, screeching and bucking, the *Sea Shepherd* came to a stop. We would pull back again and repeat the process, each time getting a few more yards deeper into the ice field.

At my request, Captain Les Fewster set a course for Havre Au Maison on the Magdalen Islands, which lay at almost dead-center in the Gulf of St. Lawrence. I had a hunch that the seal herds would be there, and the Canadian and Norwegian sealers would be moving up on them through the shifting floes.

For two days, we rammed at the ice, making progress at a snail's pace. The ice was getting thicker, and a few times we had to go over the side, shovels in hand, to dig out the *Sea Shepherd*. She would get stuck, unable to free herself on the tug backward, and there was nothing else to do but chop her out at the bow with picks and shovels.

The Canadian Coast Guard icebreaker *Wolfe* came alongside at one point, her crew at the rail jeering and making obscene hand movements. We had been checking her and any other Canadian Coast Guard facilities we could raise by radio, asking about ice conditions. It finally dawned on us that we were being fed erroneous information. To get the correct data, all we had to do after that was ask the questions, reverse the answers, and there we had it—on target!

We asked the *Wolfe* to break ice for us. Her captain refused out of hand. Some of the newsmen aboard the *Sea Shepherd* laughed at my request, one of them saying, "After all, why should they? You're the enemy!" But I did not feel that way at all. Surely, if the *Wolfe* could break ice for a Norwegian sealer, she could break ice for us, a British-registered vessel owned by a Canadian who had served in the Coast Guard himself. Lew Fewster was outraged. He vowed to push ahead with renewed intensity, to reach the seals without help from the *Wolfe*, if for no other reason than to have the last laugh.

On the morning of March 8, David MacKenney woke me up with a radio message he had intercepted from the sealing ship *Brandal.* The message indicated she was quite near. Later in the day, what appeared to be the *Brandal* showed up on our radar. But Captain Fewster, who had already reaped some revenge by breaking through the ice so fast that the *Wolfe* at one time was running behind us (we were breaking ice for the icebreaker!), thought the radar blip might be the Canadian Coast Guard vessel instead.

"Is that you?" he asked the *Wolfe* by radio.

Silence for a while, and then, like a question at a tea party, the *Wolfe* radioed,

"One blip or two?"

"Just one."

Quickly, then, the *Wolfe* said,

"That's not us."

That was all the information we needed. In trying to throw us off, the *Wolfe* had confirmed for us that she was with another vessel. What else could the other ship be but a sealer? It was only a matter of time until we could get our bearings and go into action.

We headed for the blip. As we drew closer, the one blip became two, and the two became three. It was the *Wolfe,* all right, and beside her were two sealing ships. They were in the middle of the seal pack, and we were heading toward them. For a couple of days, it seemed, we had been twenty or thirty miles away, pounding at the ice, not knowing where we wanted to go, and all the while the *Wolfe* had been watching us on her radar, holding back the secret of where she was and where the sealers were. We were elated. Nobody was happier than Les Fewster. To him, he had won a personal, one-on-one match with the captain of the *Wolfe,* his uncooperative and derisive counterpart.

Fewster drove the ship relentlessly into the ever-thickening plates of ice. The *Sea Shepherd* would land with a shuddering crash, screech hideously as the engines revved to full throttle, come to a halt, pull back, and do it again.

A few minutes before midnight, we rammed a huge block of ice and stopped with a resounding *clump*! Once more, we were wedged securely into the ice. We went for the picks and shovels, only to realize we really did not want to pull out. Off about four miles, we could see the lights of the *Wolfe* and two sealing ships. All around us we could hear the crying and whining of thousands of seals, a chorus of distress calls made all the more eerie by the other-worldliness of our surroundings—white in all directions but for the faint shadows in the Arctic mists of the ships and the seals.

We had arrived. Despite all the dire warnings, all the natural and man-made obstructions, we had made it. We had come 400 miles through the ice—the last 250 miles through a seemingly impenetrable barrier four feet thick, as solid and tough as marble—and we had come, not to kill seals, but to save them. No other ship I thought had ever done as much in such a cause.

I was first off the ship to the icepack. I went over the side amidships by rope ladder, leaping most of the way, and ran forward of the bow for about eight feet. There, a baby harp seal reposed, looking up at me with that wide-eyed, quizzical innocence that I had grown so used to seeing in 1977 and 1978. Awkwardly, wailing a protest, the pup backed away, all the while trying to keep me in sight. I followed, stooping over to lay a hand on his back, and, when he had calmed down, I stroked the smooth, white pelt that was the cause of all the furor.

I picked up the pup and took him back with me to the *Sea Shepherd* to meet the press. We sprayed a little red dye on his back and rubbed it in. It would do him no harm. It was indelible dye, bright, blood red, of the kind used to color *batik* fabrics in Java and elsewhere. It rendered the beautiful white hide a mottled mess, at least in commercial terms, until the three-week-old pup would age another three weeks and nature would darken his coat to the blackish gray of his maturity.

We returned the pup to the ice, after duly recording him on film, and I led the ice crew off the *Sea Shepherd* for wholesale spraying. This crew of eight—Mark Sterk, Keith Krueger, David MacKenney, Paul Pezwick, Eddy Smith, Joe Goodwin, and Matt Herron (who was loaded down with cameras, making pictures for *Geo* and *Penthouse* magazines as well as carrying out his seal-interference duties), and me—started out with three-foot-high, tank-type garden sprays, either held by hand or strapped to the back. But the brass nozzles kept clogging in the cold, and the tanks proved burdensome. We soon found the best method was simply to fill up a hand-held plastic spray bottle and let fly. We hopped from ice pan to ice pan, jumping over the "leads" that opened up between them, without falling into the water, and we sprayed about 150 harp seal pups.

Except for Matt Herron, the reporters would not get off the ship. They called me foolhardy for setting out so late in the day across the ice for the main body of seals in the area of the sealing ships and the Coast Guard icebreaker. The Fund for Animals people wanted to wait for the cover of darkness, when we could spray the seals and still have time to return to the safety of our ship, to avoid capture and be able to issue our own statements and news bulletins to the reporters.

David MacKenney, our thirty-second crew member (having come aboard the night before we sailed, begging to be given any assignment, as long as he could go along), was all fired up for the night-time sortie. I gained tremendous respect for him, and for the others in our ice crew. They were all for it, agreeing that we go ahead, simply because nobody expected us to. In the morning, as soon as there was daylight, they knew, as well as I did, that we would be arrested under the Seal Protection Act for interfering with the seal hunt.

If any of those on the ships had peered out across

the ice that midnight, they would have seen what must have looked like an invasion force from Mars. All in orange and hooded, with only our eyes and noses showing, we hopped from jiggling ice floe to jiggling ice flow, pausing only long enough to spray red dye on wide-eyed little seals. Wobbling about with the aid of seven-foot staffs made from the ship's gaffing poles, we pushed on without respite.

Over the first couple of miles, the seals were fairly well scattered. They were difficult to spot among the bumps, dents, and crevices, white against white in the darkness, and we did not want to miss any. There was much evidence of the sealers' handiwork. We could see the dark red remains of those seals already felled by the clubs and stripped of their pelts, heads bashed in and intestines trailing from beneath ribs.

We wanted to spray as many seals as we could, but we were concentrating, moving slowly, checking everywhere. It was methodical work, a slow-motion race against the dawn. Keith Krueger recalled later, in his personal journal, that some of us started crying as soon as we let our guard down enough to contemplate the stupidity and horror of it all. Yet we had this consolation: we saved the lives of about a thousand seals that night.

As the sun began to lighten the sky, Keith was close to exhaustion. He began to talk to the seals, cooing assurances as he splashed dye on them. At one pup, he stopped for a few minutes. There was something about the way the animal looked at him, turning his head away and cringing, as if expecting to be murdered. Keith threw on some dye and gently massaged it into the hide, like a mother giving salve to a frightened child.

"There, there, little seal," he said. "We hope we're

going to make you live. I hope you do, and grow up to see that the world's not as bad as it looks to you now. Not all humans are as bad as what you're seeing in the first days of your life."

Keith rubbed in another splash of red dye. He was talking to himself now, and to all of his fellow men. He did not find it strange that the pup was relaxing, seemed less afraid, seemed even to sense his feelings and to listen to his voice.

"This red dye will protect you, little seal. What happens is that they will see it and pass you by. And then, in a few weeks, you won't be white any more and they won't want you."

Keith began to cry as he talked. The sound of his voice on the misty Arctic air, with dawn coming up, his fierce fatigue weighing him down, the helplessness of the seals, his own jumble of thoughts—all of these filled him with a melancholy that spilled over into tears.

"I hope you survive, little friend. You need to survive. We'll help. Grow up and have babies in a better world."

And then the sun was up. From all around us came the whirring of helicopters, six of them, seemingly out of nowhere. They must have come from the Magdalen Islands, about forty miles away. We knew that the *Wolfe* carried only one or two helicopters. They skimmed along the ice, flying contour. Those that set down near us disgorged officers of the Fisheries Ministry, Quebec Provincial Police, and Royal Canadian Mounted Police (RCMP).

In charge, we learned later, was Stanley Dudka, the Fisheries Ministry official responsible for the Gulf of St. Lawrence area. He was in civilian clothes, a big and burly man, and he appeared to be very agitated. He was yelling at us to stop, shouting "bastards" and other obscenities as he came toward us.

"Come on!" I hollered to Mark Sterk, and we ran into a natural ice cave. Out of sight, we could hear all the commotion as our colleagues, scattered across the ice and spraying dye on seals to the end, were arrested and marched away.

First to be apprehended were David MacKenney, Paul Pezwick, and Eddy Smith, who had been working together more or less as a team. Keith Krueger was next, and then Joe Goodwin.

Keith was hopping about when the lawmen came up, trying to spray a large number of pups he had discovered huddled along a pressure ridge. As he worked, he was talking to himself, urging himself on.

"Come on, legs, stretch!" he said. "I need speed. I'm here, little seals! Spray, spray them all! So many. So many. Here's one behind the ridge. Christ! He's skinned! There's three over there. Spray! Spray!"

And then he was surrounded. He felt euphoric. Somebody grabbed him by the elbow.

"What's your name?"

"Keith Krueger. What's yours?"

"RCMP."

It took the officials about ten minutes to locate Mark and me in the cave. Flushed from our hiding place, we ran in opposite directions as the police reached out to take us physically into custody. Dudka, the local Fisheries Ministry boss, chased after me. I jumped aboard a small ice floe in the middle of a lead, precariously twisting and tilting to keep my balance with the help of my seven-foot-long balancing stick.

Dudka stopped at the edge of the lead, pointed to my stick, and yelled at a uniformed Mountie:

"Shoot that man! He's armed!"

The officer looked at Dudka, looked at me, and did nothing. For the moment, I was safe on my block of ice in the middle of my tiny pond.

Matt Herron, who had been straggling behind, taking closeup photographs of the baby seals, came running and scrambling over the ice. He was muttering curses, damning himself for having missed the chance to photograph our captures. The police grabbed him and put an end to photographing.

Dudka stood at the edge of the lead, glowering at me.

"Big hero!" he shouted. "Standing out there in the middle of the lead! Big hero! Gonna resist arrest! You want a medal?"

"You going to give me one?"

"We're going to send you up for the rest of your life!"

"That's up to you."

He was sputtering with rage, shaking his fist at me. He picked up Matt Herron's balancing staff and poked me in the ribs, again and again. Later I could hardly move for the pain in those ribs. The pain was almost unbearable, sharp, like a shot of electricity. I did not know how to avoid his jabs. If I dodged too quickly or too far, I would fall off my block of ice. When he jabbed again, I swung my own stick, breaking his staff into three pieces, which fell into the water.

One of the helicopters came over and practically landed on my head. The pilot brought it down slowly, and it seemed to me he was trying to push me down and off the ice. Crouching, I thrust my stick upward, toward the whirring rotor blades. Like a jackrabbit popping from a burrow, the chopper jumped about twenty-five feet into the air and moved away.

By now, I had attracted a pretty good crowd. Dudka had about twenty-five officers surrounding the patch of water in which I had marooned myself on a miniature iceberg. What now? I wondered if somebody might find another stick and start poking at me again. I began to think I would be back in the frigid water again, as in my 1977 brush with the sealers, and that might mean another bout with pneumonia.

Out of the corner of my eye, I saw a flash of something dark, and I instinctively dodged. A body went hurtling by me and splashed into the water. A flying tackle on the ice? A rash move! And he paid for his rashness.

As I was fending off somebody else, a Quebec policeman dove across the lead and tackled me, and we both toppled into the water. He was helped out, and I clambered back on my little ice pan. I was soaking wet and beginning to shiver. I took out my camera from around my neck, and started to throw it to Matt Herron, but Dudka picked up a stick, making as if to bat down the camera. I held on to it.

Mark Sterk, handcuffed and manhandled, was shoved into a helicopter and flown to the *Wolfe*. From the lead, I made pictures of that.

"You'll never see that photograph," Dudka snarled.

Mounties and Fisheries officers tried to lasso me with a rope, but I used my staff to fend it off. I had been out there at bay for twenty minutes or so when the police figured out how to get me. Two men stretched a rope across the lead, one holding one end and one holding the other. They walked, holding the rope taut between them. I fought, but the rope skimmed me off the pan like a hockey stick swatting a hockey puck.

As the police dragged me onto the ice, Dudka hopped up and down on my fingers. I heard later he was so furious because he had promised Fisheries Minister Roméo LeBlanc that not a single seal would be sprayed.

"Resist me, will you?" he yelled. "Resist me, and I'll kill you!"

Dudka was kicking me, landing solid blows in my side, as the Mounties pulled me up higher on the ice and struggled to put handcuffs on me. Somebody tied my feet together, and then my manacled hands were tied to my ankles. Lifted up by the handcuffs, I was thrown into the helicopter, transported to the *Wolfe,* pulled out and dragged, again by the handcuffs, across the helicopter pad to a wardroom, where the ropes that bound my hands to my feet were removed.

In the wardroom was the rest of the ice team. All seven were sitting around, bedraggled, with most of their clothes off. Joe Goodwin, who had put up considerable resistance when apprehended, was still in handcuffs.

"You come with me," a Mountie said, grabbing me by the hair.

As I tried to resist, Joe came flying out of his chair, handcuffs and all, and dove headlong into the Mountie. Since my hands were manacled, behind my back, I had trouble fighting off the man. With others soon helping him, he dragged me to the forepeak and threw me down on the forward main deck. When I tried to get up, a Mountie kicked me in the back. I tried again, and he kicked again, and so I stayed down, waiting to see what would happen next.

My wet clothes had long frozen. My hands were going numb. I was miserable and cold, shivering and aching all over. I tried a third time to get to my feet, and once more the Mountie kicked me in the back.

For two and a half hours, according to those in the wardroom, I lay on the deck, face down, hands cuffed behind, wishing for something to happen to remove the pain. I was only dimly aware of the Mounties standing around me. They seemed to be speaking only in French. I could hear a laugh now and then. When I moved, I would be kicked. I would pass out and awaken to even more intensified pain and cold.

I thought there might be a plan to see to it that I froze to death. The Mounties had not interfered in 1977, when the sealers had dunked me in the water and beaten me. What was different about the situation now was that the Mounties were in charge.

With all the strength I could muster, I raised my head and then brought it crashing down on the deck. I did not know if the strategy would work. But if I could knock myself out, maybe the pain would stop. I lifted my head again and brought it down on the deck, hard.

I was grabbed and shaken roughly.

"What the hell do you think you are doing? Are you crazy?"

Was I crazy? Was *I* crazy? What about *them?*

"Have you had enough, English?" the Mountie taunted, leaning over me. "Do you think you will return to the ice next year? Do you?"

I could hardly speak, but I managed to groan:

"No."

"Good," he said. "If you do return, next time we'll kill you."

Dragged back across the deck, I was returned to the wardroom. Matt Herron demanded blankets and hot coffee or tea for me. The Mounties refused. He asked for the ship's doctor, and he was told there was none. His fury mounting, Matt helped Keith Krueger strip me of my frozen clothes. They rubbed me to restore my circulation. The numbness began to fade, and, as it did, my body felt as if it were on fire.

Soon, the Mounties came back and dragged me to the helicopter for the flight to the Magdalen Islands and jail. Looking down as we flew over the seal pack, I could see the clubs rising and falling, with the familiar streaks of red on the ice. I closed my eyes to shut out the sight, and I fell sound asleep.

With a scream I came wide awake. A Mountie had me by the handcuffs again, and the pain against both wrists as he twisted and turned was almost unbearable. The bony parts of my wrists were raw already, and I wondered how I could stand any more pain in such parts of my body that had already been abused.

I was pulled out of the helicopter to the ground. I had the feeling I was in the midst of a large crowd, perhaps thirty or forty men, and they all seemed to be laughing at me. The Mountie struck me across the back three times with what I took to be a rubber hose. Each time, the crowd cheered and clapped.

I was taken by car to a hospital, where a doctor gave me a quick examination, I then was driven to a jail and locked in a cell. I was in Cap Aux Meulles in the Magdalens, among pro-sealers who hated the likes of me.

My companions were hauled in one by one. Keith Krueger was first, followed by Matt Herron, and then the others. The Fisheries Ministry was using one helicopter per demonstrator, and each newcomer had to run the gauntlet of abuse set up outside the jail by local sealer sympathizers. When meal-time came, they served us seal-meat stew, and made sure we knew what it was. We did not eat it, of course.

All eight of us were charged with violating the Seal

Protection Act, resisting arrest, assaulting police officers, and obstructing justice. Two by two, we were taken to a courtroom in the same building. Dudka and a contingent of Mounties were there, pressing charges. Cleveland Amory, was also there, with Jacques Laurin, a lawyer he had brought in from Montreal. It was all pretty cut and dried. Dudka testified I hit him with a lead pipe, and, when I blurted out that he could show no bruise, the judge threatened me with a contempt citation if I did not keep quiet. Our bail was set at sixteen thousand dollars and our trial for August 6, 1979. Cleveland Amory promised the money, and, as always, was true to his word.

In the meantime, some of the news people had a hard time of it, too. A score of sealer sympathizers, after a few drinks, assaulted four of the newsmen who had been aboard the *Sea Shepherd.* None of the tormentors spoke English, and so they could not understand the protests that their victims were news people and not activists. They poured wine over the heads of the four, spray-painted large red crosses on their clothes, and held them hostage for seven harrowing hours.

Cleveland Amory and his Fund for Animals staff, along with Frank Milner of the Royal Society for the Prevention of Cruelty to Animals and Sunny Lewis of Vancouver's radio station CHUM/CFUN, also suffered a roughing-up as they left Magdalen Islands by air. Sunny reported later that, when the group arrived at the airport terminal, it "looked more like an armed camp." She added,

"The Islanders were all sitting outside around the building in their cars, getting drunk and hating us. Inside there was a Customs man and one RCMP officer to make sure things didn't get on too ugly a front. When four guys came into the building and approached us just before our plane arrived I thought there was going to be a fight for sure. But they let us go without any more trouble. . . .

"It seems as if the Canadian government allows these people to be as brutal as they like—seals or people, what's the difference? The protection of the government goes to the aggressor."

As soon as we had been taken prisoner, Dudka went by helicopter to the *Sea Shepherd* to order our ship off the ice. Canadian Coast Guard help was denied, even though Captain Les Fewster explained that he was stuck in the ice and his Loran gear was not working. With the eight of us in jail, Cleveland Amory and his staff and our London sponsor gone, as well as the dozen news media personnel, the captain had very few bodies around to man his ship. But he moved her, at great peril and with great skill, to Sydney, Nova Scotia. Repairs were made there, and the *Sea Shepherd* stood by for us, ready for the return trip to Boston.

Tina Harrison from Vancouver, armed with the Fund for Animal's sixteen-thousand-dollar check for bail money, got us out of jail on March 14, 1979. We were free, after five days imprisonment, but we still had to get off the island. The scheduled airline between the Magdalens and Charlottetown on Prince Edward Island refused to take us because of a telephoned threat from the Magdalens that any plane carrying us would be bombed. The Mounties and the Quebec Provincial Police declined help. We turned again to Cleveland Amory as our savior. We reached his assistant, Marian Probst, who sent a chartered aircraft to pick us up. It had taken forty-five telephone calls, Marian told us later, before she found an air charter company willing to risk going for us.

Unfortunately, a five-seater was all that was available. Matt Herron, Keith Krueger, Tina Harrison, and I agreed to be in "the second wave." The other five, escorted by Quebec Provincial Police officers, went to the airport, about twenty miles from the jail, and took off for Charlottetown without incident.

However, on an island populated by Citizens Band radio buffs, everybody who cared knew what was happening. Matt Herron, who had covered civil rights disturbances in the American South, said the aura of tension and entrapment was extraordinarily familiar. "If it wasn't for the snow and tundra," he said, "this place could be Mississippi."

We four walked out of the jail together, I got into one police car with Matt. Keith and Tina slid into another. We took different routes to the airport. It was a dark and cloudy night, with a fitful moon.

At the airport, as we waited for the plane to return for us, we could feel it happening. Automobiles, with three and four men in them, began quietly pulling into the parking lot. The men sat in their cars, holding baseball bats and cans of paint, and stared malevolently.

One of the officers escorting us took a firm grip on his nightstick and went over to the cars. He stopped at one whose occupants seemed particularly vigorous in displaying their baseball bats. He leaned over and talked to them earnestly in French. They grunted back a few words, and he returned to us, walking quickly. He said something in French, excitedly, to the officer at the wheel of the car bearing Tina and Keith. Then he hopped into our car beside the driver and said, *"Allons, vite!"* Even I knew that meant for us to get out of there in a hurry, and that is what we did. The other car, with Tina and Keith in it, was right behind us. And behind them was a long line of headlights, following just as fast.

Suddenly, our car turned off the road, sped between two sheds, and skidded to a halt between a couple of old, beached fishing boats. The officer turned off his lights. The other patrol car passed by our hiding place and, as we learned later, found a hiding place of its own.

About thirty sedans, pickups, vans, and land rovers went sailing by in convoy, none of them, apparently, aware of where we were. It was all pretty ridiculous—the police hiding from the populace.

Down the road, as we headed back for the airport, we came upon a Fisheries Ministry land rover parked in such a way as to command a full view of the airport road. We stopped, and our police, after checking, told us that the Fisheries employee in the land rover was reporting our position via CB radio. So we knew that our friends with the paint cans and baseball bats would soon be on their way back.

At the airport once more, we could see the lights of the small plane descending to the runway. The two police cars drove out on the Tarmac just as the mob arrived in its motley collection of vehicles. We jumped out and jogged toward the still-moving plane. As my three companions were scrambling onto the wing and into the cabin, and just as I turned to join them, the Quebec Provincial Police officer who had been my driver shouted wryly above the roar of the engine, "I hope you enjoyed your stay on our beautiful, friendly island." I laughed, reached out and shook his hand, turned for one last look at the Magdalens, and climbed aboard the moving aircraft.

Not fifty yards away, through the snow that had begun to fall with increasing intensity, I saw the mob. Enraged at having missed their quarry, screaming and waving their buckets and bats, the men came at a dead run. As I settled into the plane with the others, I felt sudden movement. The engines roared. The snow outside my window began to bend and then fly past in ribbons of white. In moments, we were aloft and free.

We stopped briefly at Charlottetown, to let Tina Harrison off and to confer with Cleveland Amory, and went on from there to Sydney, Nova Scotia, and the *Sea Shepherd*. From Sydney to Boston, we sailed with a severely reduced crew. But it was only two days, and, after all we had been through, that went by quickly and easily. In Boston, we had more sad goodbyes, to Keith Krueger, Joe Goodwin, Mark Sterk, and Eddy Smith, who had jobs and other commitments elsewhere. But Paul Pezwick and David MacKenney stayed on, and we started to rebuild for the next outing.

Les Fewster agreed to my request that he remain as captain. My father decided on his own to stay, and he brought in a friend from British Columbia named Alexander Hamilton as first mate, whom I accepted. I signed on as second mate, and we had a few other additions, including a couple of women, Terri Silvain and Barbara Lynn-Motes, to help Starlet in the galley. Applicants for crew slots were coming in almost daily, thanks to all the publicity we had received locally while on the ice. Screening to make selections was a tedious and time-consuming process for me.

The hundred-dollar-a-day dock fee was killing our budget, and we figured we might do better, as a British-registered vessel, in a British port. Bermuda was about the closest, and Bermuda it was. We cleared port and, for the entire three-day trip, sailed in abominable weather.

One day out, we were hit by a force-eight gale. Most of the crew went down with seasickness, although the three old hands—Captain Fewster, Mate Hamilton, and my father, the cook—seemed to enjoy the storm while sharing a bottle on the bridge.

"It's starting to freshen up a wee bit, I think," the captain would announce with the regularity of a buoy bell, and the other two, between nips, would nod agreement and laugh uproariously.

At one particularly rough point, Al Johnson went sailing across the bridge and cracked his head open on the ship's brass telegraph. Bandaged, back on watch, Al was as philosophical as the skipper, the mate, and my father.

"It's a dirty job," he kept saying, with mock sighs of dutiful resignation, "but somebody's got to do it."

12

Stalking the Pirate

BERMUDA WAS PARADISE after the ice of Newfoundland and the cold of Boston. Bouncing out of the storm, we were beside ourselves with joy at the sight of the neat, sunny houses of St. George and the genteel bustle of its port—busy, but not with unseemly intensity, as befits a sub-tropical community, and one run by the British at that. We tied up at a rickety old dock, cleared customs, and immediately leaped overboard *en masse* for a cleansing, warming swim in the clear water of the harbor. People on shore looked amazed, pointing and laughing at us. Here it was, only March 22, and we were jumping in the water. No Bermudian in his right mind goes swimming before the last week in May.

Having come south partly to escape Boston's hundred-dollar-per-day dock fee, we were less than thrilled when Norman Roberts, the mayor of St. George, told us that the price of using his dock would be one hundred dollars per day. We argued that we were noncommercial, had no way of generating revenue, and should not be required to pay the same docking fee as vessels able to earn their way. He was adamant, and we had no choice but to accept his terms.

We were assigned a berth with no water or waste-disposal facilities, and the dock itself, dangerously in need of repair, was unsafe to walk on. Moreover, every time a commercial ship appeared, we were ordered out to anchor, which meant paying a pilot's fee, until unloading and loading were accomplished. After about two weeks, we were shifted to a berth alongside a rusty freighter, the *Dania,* of Panamanian registry, that had been chased into Bermuda by the U.S. Coast Guard. She was suspected of carrying drugs from Morocco. Having been challenged off the coast of North Carolina, she fled from U.S. waters, blowing her boilers in the chase; she had exhausted her fresh water and pumped in sea water for the engines. After all this, Bermuda authorities found nothing on her to confiscate.

The Bermuda government, embarrassed by this leaky, evil-smelling old tub sitting in port, offered us a full load of fuel if we would haul the *Dania.*

"Where to?" I asked.

"Anywhere," the port official replied. "Just get her the bloody hell out of here."

"Okay," I said, "I'll haul her out and sink her."

"No, no, no," he said. "You can't do that. You must take her somewhere."

"Where?"

There was no ready answer to this, and the *Dania* remained in port, becoming more disreputable by the day as her crew members drifted away. Just before we shifted to another berth, she was down to about four Pakistanis who stood guard against vandals. Otherwise, she was deserted, except for the rats. We hated having to walk across her deck to reach the dock.

The mystery of the *Dania*'s cargo was never officially solved, but about three months after she showed up in St. George's harbor, great bales of marijuana were washed up on Bermuda's shores.

Our fortunes took a turn for the better after some Bermudian friends, Sam and Elizabeth Merse-Brown, interceded with the British Royal Navy establishment on our behalf. We were allowed to tie up, at no cost, in an unused part of the Royal Navy Dockyard. As if by magic, other good things followed. The Bermuda Paint Company donated some Navy gray paint, which turned the dark hull of the *Sea Shepherd* into the body of a sleek and graceful dove, and others on the island came forward with help, financial or otherwise. They included enlisted men at the American armed forces base; Bishop Anselm Genders, the Anglican Bishop of Bermuda; David Wingate, the Bermuda government's conservation officer; members of the Bermuda police force; and British sailors at the dockyard.

Three nuclear submarines arrived—two U.S. Navy and the other British—and we showed films of our fight for the seals aboard one of them. The British Navy's flagship, the carrier *Intrepid,* appeared, as did a number of Canadian vessels on maneuvers. We toured some of these ships and made friends. We learned then that the Canadian government, through aerial reconnaissance, had kept very close watch over the *Sea Shepherd*. The Canadian-marked aircraft that had circled over us so frequently, while we searched for the sealing fleet, were indeed recording our position and taking our picture.

I could not resist saying, "We could have saved the government a lot of money. For a small commission, we would have been glad to radio our position every day, and all those overflights would not have been necessary, not to mention all the police staked out from one end of the Gulf of St. Lawrence to the other."

The governor of Bermuda received us one evening, and I spent much of my time giving talks to various groups—the English Speaking Union, Rotary Clubs, a Lions Club, the Policeman's Club, the Diving Club, the Folk Singer's Club, the Audubon Society, and the Society for the Prevention of Cruelty to Animals—as well as spreading our message through interviews for radio, television, and newspapers. Everything was going beautifully. But then the backlash set in.

A Bermuda dentist in a newspaper interview attacked us as fanatics undermining the Canadian seal industry. An undertaker from Newfoundland, who said he was in Bermuda on vacation, also denounced us, saying we had faked the films of seal-killing. A Presbyterian minister, a Newfoundlander, said Bermudians might lose their coveted codfish at breakfast time if seals were not killed before they ate the cod, and the Roman Catholic bishop suggested to his Anglican colleague that he withdraw his support from us. Bishop Genders' response was to come out and bless our ship with holy water. Fortunately, our critics were in the minority. However, despite the continuing hospitality of most Bermudians, it began to sink in that we probably were wasting our time, albeit amid very pleasant surroundings. We had to think about moving on.

In early June, Cleveland Amory flew to Bermuda to discuss the future of the *Sea Shepherd* in his plans for Fund for Animals activism. He said he wanted me to sail immediately to the Bering Sea to stage a protest against the U.S.-sponsored killing of fur seals by Aleuts in the Pribilof Islands. The annual hunt was scheduled to begin, as usual, in July, and there was just enough time for us to make it. However, the cost of getting there, via the Panama Canal, would be high.

But it was not the cost that turned me away from any Pribilof campaign. I wanted to shift now to fighting for whales. I wanted to go after the most infamous whaler then operating, the *Sierra,* and I wanted that more than anything else in the world. I felt we could demonstrate our power and dedication with dramatic impact by showing versatility—saving seals in the Gulf of Labrador in the spring, and then saving whales in the Atlantic in the summer. And this time, I knew, we would get maximum world attention when I rammed the *Sierra* with the *Sea Shepherd.*

Cleveland was hesitant, and I knew why. At sixty-three, he was a tough, courageous veteran of many a conservation campaign. He had proven many times that he would not hesitate to take professional and personal risks. However, what I was asking put a heavy burden on him. A high-seas attack on another ship was a far cry from the nonviolent defense of animals, and he was wary of the risks—to the good name of his organization and to the safety and well-being of those of us who would carry out the mission. It was not possible for him to come along, because of his other commitments, and I was asking for more—for his blessing and for support in an admitted gamble that could end in disaster.

I knew, as we talked in Bermuda, of his doubts. I also knew that he hated the pirate whalers as much as I did; he wanted the seas rid of them—a step toward the eradication of all whaling. It was on that point that I concentrated.

"I want the *Sierra* stopped, Cleveland," I pleaded. "She's out there on this ocean somewhere. I want to stop her."

He lowered his eyes and shook his head slowly.

"I don't know."

"Let me try, Cleveland. Let me try. If it doesn't work, I'll sell the *Sea Shepherd* in Spain. Let me go after her. . . ."

He shook his head again, more forcefully this time.

"You'll never find her. The Atlantic is a big ocean. You'll never find the *Sierra*. And then stopping her? No, the chances are too remote, and there's a helluva lot of money involved. I don't know if I can justify committing the Fund to taking chances like this. . . ."

I was losing the argument, I could see. I could argue that we had found the sealers off Newfoundland three times, with officials trying hard to throw us off. I could argue that we had found the Russian whalers in the Pacific on two occasions—three, really, counting the two confrontations in 1976 as separate expeditions. But I could see that I would have to try again with Amory at some later date, when I could marshal more data in support of what was now little more than a "gut feeling" that I could find the *Sierra* and put her out of action.

"Let me work on it, then," I said. "Let me keep you posted while I put together more information. Please don't make a decision yet. Don't reject this idea until I have had a chance to show you in more detail why I think I can do it. Give me some time. Give me a month."

He watched me carefully. We had worked together for a while now, and he knew me as well as any man. He nodded. Okay, a month it was.

I was now in pretty good shape. I had two strong supporters—Cleveland Amory, the president of the Fund for Animals, and Lewis Regenstein, the Fund's vice president, in charge of the Washington, D.C., office. "Speaking just for myself, Paul," Lew had said, "I'd like to give you torpedoes. Sink the son of a bitch, if you can."

Although I spoke confidently when seeking to rally support or recruit crew members, in my heart I was pretty close to panic. Where was the *Sierra?* If I did not have a precise fix, where would I start looking? What would I do for a crew? What would I do, if and when I did find the *Sierra?* And, long before then, where would I begin to look for information on the *Sierra*—her habits and her likely whereabouts? I telephoned two old friends in Greenpeace. One said he was too busy to help—he was planning a walkathon fund-raiser; the other, when I asked if he knew where the *Sierra* was, replied, "Perhaps, but that's classified Greenpeace information, and the *Sea Shepherd* is not a Greenpeace ship." When I argued, he added, "We don't like your tactics. We don't trust you."

"Hell," I said to myself, "I don't have a clue as to where or how to start."

The *Sea Shepherd* was a thing of beauty once more. Her battleship gray sparkled in the Bermuda sunlight. The brilliant rainbow arcing up the side of the hull just forward of amidships provided an unexpected dash of color. She looked trim, proud, strong, and right at home among the British Royal Navy ships at the Royal Navy Dockyard. A nice touch, I thought, was the British red ensign flapping jauntily from the guy wires atop our foremast.

I cannot possibly exaggerate how proud I was of the *Sea Shepherd.* The Fund for Animals, with some help from the Royal Society for the Prevention of Cruelty to Animals, had bought and paid for her. But she was registered in my name. I made her plans and I operated her. From a castoff, a rust-encrusted reject, retired without honors after a lifetime of dedicated service to the North Atlantic fisheries, she had been brought to what she was now: a sleek, even racy-looking protector of the life of the sea. The beauty and the poetic justice of the situation sometimes carried me away, especially when I was most distressed over the plight of the whale. My spirits would soar when I recalled how far we had come with the *Sea Shepherd.* Beneath the rust and scales, I had seen her beauty and her potential in confrontation, too, that first day that I boarded her at Hull in Yorkshire, England. Had it been only six months?

The *Sea Shepherd* could do the job, I knew. She was bigger, heavier, and faster (I hoped) than the *Sierra.* We would have the advantage over the *Sierra,* just as she had the advantage over the whales. The odds would be on our side, for a change. *If* I could find the *Sierra.*

Of all the ships operating outside the International Whaling Commission's regulations, the most offensive was the *Sierra.* For more than a decade, this 683-ton catcher/factory ship had been slaughtering whales with impunity while flying various flags of convenience. Built in 1960 in Holland as a highspeed catcher boat, she worked with the Dutch factory ship *Willem Barendsz* in the Antarctic for four years, until the blue whale population collapsed and the Dutch whaling industry went bankrupt. In 1967, she was converted at a Dutch shipyard to a processor as well as killer—the rear half reconstructed to include a long deck, capable of holding several whales, with a sloping stern slipway for hauling the whales aboard. Below, a quick-freezing plate and huge freezer compartments were installed. She had become a one-ship whaling fleet, convenience-registered in the Bahamas.

From 1968 to 1971, her harpoons feasted on 1,676 whales, mostly of the Bryde's species, but also humpbacks and the very rare southern right whales. The meat was shipped to Japan. In 1971, the Bahamian government withdrew its registration and levied a heavy fine for various violations of regulations—a fine that was never paid. In liquidation proceedings in South Africa, the ship was taken over by a Norwegian bank, Forretningsbanken of Trondheim, which held the mortgage. Ownership was hidden through a South African group headed by an entrepreneur named Andrew Behr. This new operation, called Sierra Fishing and Trading Company, was first registered in Spain's Canary Islands, but in 1973 it switched to Sierra Agency in Cape Town, South Africa, with the ship registered under the flag of Somalia.

In June of 1973, Andrew Behr, as registered owner and agent for the *Sierra,* put together a contract with Taiyo Canada, Ltd., the Canadian subsidiary of Japan's Taiyo Fishery Company. The three-year agreement called for delivery of three thousand tons annually of frozen sei whale and Bryde's whalemeat at an Angolan or other African port. The frozen whalemeat, in polyurethane bags, originally produced in South Africa but later in Norway, went for 138,000 yen per metric ton. Taiyo, with Canadian headquarters in St. John's, Newfoundland, made the *Sierra* payments through the Bank of Montreal. Under the contract, Taiyo put six Japanese experts aboard to supervise the butchering, so that Japanese consumers would have their steaks cut just so. The *Sierra* killed four hundred to five hundred whales a year, working the Angolan coast until the civil war there forced it farther north. There, using the Ivory Coast capital of Abidjan to refuel and drop off its kill, which was picked up by Japanese freighters, the *Sierra* scored easily in Bryde's whale mating and calving grounds close to shore.

This outlaw ship specialized in hunting legally protected whales—critically endangered species, nursing infants, pregnant mothers—whatever whales were easi-

est to find and kill. Even among outlaw whalers, the
Sierra was notorious for ruthlessness. Once, a Nigerian
Navy gunboat surprised her after she had wiped out a
small herd of whales in a bay well within Nigerian
waters. The Nigerians held their fire as the *Sierra*, her
harpooner aiming his launcher menacingly, scooted out
to sea. As a pirate, with no restrictions on her activity,
the *Sierra* had a simple formula: Kill whales, kill them
all, down to the last nursing infant. Andrew Behr, in a
1975 news interview, defended this philosophy as of little moment amid the inevitable, saying, "There can be
no doubt about the fact that whales are doomed to
extinction."

The *Sierra* captain in 1979 was Arvid Nordengen,
then fifty-one. The mate and harpooner was Knut
Hustvedt, then fifty. Both, like the bank secretly owning
the ship, were Norwegian—a fact that, when it became
known publicly, proved embarrassing to the Norwegian
government. The harpoons aboard the *Sierra* were Norwegian, too, produced by Kongsberg Vapenfabrikk—a
plant west of Oslo that is owned by the Norwegian government. It also produces military equipment. In whaling's heyday, this firm turned out harpoons, grenades,
harpoon shafts, and harpoon launchers; it still does,
although in lesser volume, along with two other Norwegian subcontractors, H. Henriksen Mekanisk
Verksted and Lorentzen Mekanisk Verksted. As its
notoriety spread, the *Sierra* stopped reporting its catch
in 1978. Norway denied involvement, and in May 1979,
a spokesman for the Norwegian embassy in Washington
blurted out that his government knew for a fact that
"the *Sierra* is owned by the Japanese."

The Japanese connection had long been an open
secret. The United States, which had been buying from

Japan about a half-billion dollars worth of fish every year, was reluctant to upset trade relations with Japan by pressing the Japanese on their whaling excesses. But the case was thoroughly documented in U.S. Senate hearings in Washington in 1979. Taiyo purchased partial ownership in the *Sierra* in 1974, through a dummy company set up in Liechtenstein, where dummy corporations are a thriving industry. Taiyo was an old hand at that. This multinational giant, the sixty-seventh largest industrial corporation outside the United States, has eighty-three affiliates and subsidiaries in Japan and twenty-nine subsidiaries and partnerships in twenty-two countries overseas. Annual sales total more than $6 billion. It is the largest privately owned fishing company in the world, with more than 350 ships of its own and another 76 under lease. Founded in 1880, it dominates the Japanese fishing industry, with ties to Mitsubishi and other huge banking and trading interests in Japan. It is diversifying rapidly, adding food-processing and even shipbuilding to its activities.

Craig Van Note, of The Monitor conservation consortium, has reported that Taiyo has managed over the years to weave "an intricate web of dummy companies in such havens as Panama, Liberia, Taiwan, and Liechtenstein to hide its control of the outlaw whalers." He has assembled the following evidence, which he turned over to the U.S. Congress:

• In Peru, Taiyo owns at least 77 percent of a company operating an outlaw whaling station that kills 1,500 whales annually, owns a major share of the processing factory, and ships the frozen catch to Japan. This company built the three catcher boats being used off Peru.

• In Taiwan, the outlaw whaler *Sea Bird* was built in

a Taiyo shipyard and is operated by a Taiwanese firm believed to be connected with Taiyo. Three more whaling ships were later added to the *Sea Bird* operation.

• In Spain, Taiyo employees supervise whaling stations that export frozen whalemeat produced by outlaw operations to Japan.

• Refrigerator ships owned by Taiyo regularly picked up whalemeat from the *Sierra* and, for a time, from her sister ship, the *Tonna,* which appeared in the Canary Islands area in 1978.

The *Tonna* was built as a 563-ton stern trawler in Taiyo's Hayashinkane Shipbuilding Yard in 1966. Twelve years later, when she joined the *Sierra,* she had been converted to a factory whaling ship, working at processing while the *Sierra* did the killing. In one forty-two-day period off the coast of Senegal in West Africa, the *Sierra* harpooned 102 sei whales and the *Tonna* packed up 432 tons of frozen meat. In June of 1978, the *Sierra* docked for repairs, and the *Tonna* set out on her own, a huge harpoon gun mounted on her bow. By July 22, she was on her way back to the Canary Islands, with 450 tons of whale meat jammed inside her, causing her to ride low in the water. The lookout spotted a fin whale ahead—more than sixty feet long and seventy tons in weight, worth $15,000, carrying a promise of a bonus for each officer aboard of $2.50 per ton. It was too much to resist. The *Tonna* made the kill. But, as the whale was being hauled up the *Tonna's* rear end, it suddenly shifted against the starboard railing. The overloaded vessel lurched into a sharp list. And then a sudden squall blew up. Great waves went crashing through open portholes and into the engine room, shorting out all electrical circuits. With no power, the crew hacked frantically at the whale to rid the ship of that tremendous dead weight. But to no avail. The *Tonna* began to sink. The crew took to three lifeboats, and Captain Kristof Vesterheim, a veteran Norwegian whaler, went down with the ship.

Just before she sank, Craig Van Note observed, witnesses reported that "the *Tonna* wallowed helplessly—like a harpooned whale."

The Japanese government, like the Norwegian government, issues pious denials of involvement by Taiyo or other Japanese companies in outlaw whaling. In international meetings, such as sessions of the International Whaling Commission, Japan once opposed any efforts to ban imports of whale products from countries that are not IWC members. But Japan now bans most if not all illicit imports. Former U.S. Whaling Commissioner Richard Frank has said, of the IWC's own lack of success, "Outlaw whaling and pirate ships prosper only because we help them to prosper." In other words, the IWC would get tough if the nations that are members wanted it to.

June of 1979 was a time of final preparations for the *Sea Shepherd* to leave Bermuda to hunt down and ram the *Sierra*. Word had come from Cleveland Amory that launched those preparations. He telephoned me and said that, after thinking over my arguments, he would not stand in my way. The Royal Navy Dockyard, helpful to the end, allowed us to buy our fuel from its resources after the Shell people refused to sell us fuel. As usual, we had a few crew changes. David MacKenney, our radio operator, who had proven himself a valuable addition when we struggled on the ice, left us for a Fund for Animals expedition to record the northern fur seal hunt in the Pribilofs. Keith Krueger would be joining him from Hawaii. Leslie Smith and Charlie Ralph left. Starlet returned to Vancouver to see what she could do about raising funds. Margaret Morey, from the Boston office of the Fund for Animals, and Steve Ryan, also from Boston, came to Bermuda to help us get ready. Peter Woof came all the way from Australia to join us. Peter was a mechanical wizard, just what I needed, what with an ailing generator and other difficulties—all of which he quickly set in order. He was a complete volunteer: he had read about us and used his own money to fly over to join us.

We sailed from Bermuda to Boston, where we had the usual hassle for supplies and fuel. Putting together a crew took some time, too. But again, all things considered, we did all right.

I felt very fortunate, as expedition leader, to have David Sellers as skipper of the *Sea Shepherd*. It meant a lot to have a friend of more than a dozen years with me. In fact, he had been the first to inspire me to go to sea. With David as captain, I knew we would be able to cross the ocean without problems, and, for that matter, get to wherever we set out for. Jacques Longini, with whom I had sailed on earlier expeditions in the Pacific, was our first mate, and Bill Shober of Boston was our second. The rest of the twenty in our crew included: Peter Woof, grease on his face and a wrench in his hand, as chief engineer; Paul Pezwick and Jerry Doran as second and third engineers, respectively; Michael Louis as carpenter; Paul Condon as chief cook, with Gail Lima and Dianne Keefe as his helpers; Alex Hamilton as bosun, with Sandy Hamilton, Alex Pacheco, Kevin Babuik, and Giovanni Tondi as seamen, and Stanley Jackson, Richard Morrison, Albert Indelicato, and Perry Cattau as oiler/wipers in the engine room.

The weather was calm and cool, the seas were smooth. We eased out of our berth in Boston on July 3, 1979, at 4:15 P.M. and set a course for the Azores. The best information I had was that the *Sierra* was operating off the coast of North Africa. According to my informant, conservationist leader Craig Van Note, she probably would head almost immediately for Oporto in Portugal to unload—and that is where I intended to take the *Sea Shepherd* for a confrontation. Van Note's organization in Washington, D.C., had developed intelligence sources throughout the world, and his reports on the *Sierra* to me were an unexpected windfall.

We arrived at Horta in the Azores early on the morning of July 12. Our plan was to take on provisions and water. Soon after we docked, a small open whaler left the harbor with a crew armed with lances and hand-held harpoons. We were told they were off to hunt down a sperm whale that had been seen near shore. They wanted the whale's teeth, to sell to tourists. The rest of the whale was to be left to rot at sea. The whalers returned empty-handed in a couple of hours, filed into a tavern, and drank themselves dizzy.

We managed a fairly early departure the next day from Horta; I was impatient to make a beeline for Oporto. A couple of weeks had passed since our last report on the pirate whaler, but I felt the *Sierra* might still be within our range. At the same time I was pessimistic, even gloomy, and was developing some secret doubts as to whether the *Sea Shepherd* was a sound conservationist investment. Fuel was fiendishly expensive, getting up a solid crew was exceedingly difficult, and the whole responsibility weighed heavily.

On that Friday, July 13, 1979, with the sea so flat and glassy it looked like a vast lagoon, we had several small adventures. The first was the sighting of a solo sailor in a small boat, the *Silver Lady,* bound for England. We asked him if he needed anything. Back came the answer, "Negative," and he continued happily on his way. Later we stopped the *Sea Shepherd* to give Peter Woof a chance to work on an ailing pump, and all of us frolicked in the ocean with a large collection of sea turtles, hundreds of them. The sea was alive with turtles and other creatures that day. For a couple of hours, we swam among the turtles, playing with them and being as friendly with them as they would allow. Many dolphins came around and an occasional shark lounged on the surface nearby. It was a joyful interlude, especially for the landlubbers among our crew, who were flabbergasted.

We took advantage of the respite to blow up and launch our V-hulled Avon inflatable boat. When the ship was underway again, I took a crew volunteer, Sandy Hamilton, for a few runs across the bow, maneuvering as we had with the Zodiac *kamikazes* out in front of the Soviet whalers, to get between the harpoon cannon and the whales being pursued. Sandy caught one of the smaller turtles by hand and we took it back to the ship to have its picture taken before returning it to the sea. After that, I gave two other volunteer crew members, Gail Lima and Giovanni Tondi, a ride out in front of the bow.

On the day we swam with the turtles, I learned later, my old friend, David Garrick, was in South Dakota talking about our expedition with another old friend, Leonard Crow Dog, the Oglala Sioux holy man and medicine man. David, or Two Deer Lone Eagle (his tribal name), had asked Leonard Crow Dog for guidance and support on our behalf. Would the holy man pray for the *Sea Shepherd*'s success and safety? And for the safety of Gray

Wolf Clear Water (my tribal name)? I was, as I had vowed in the sweat lodge, doing my utmost to save the whales, David said. Would Leonard Crow Dog invoke blessings on our mission?

The Indian mystic closed his eyes and threw back his head. David heard him mumbling, almost as if to himself. It was a private ceremony, and David sat in complete silence, respectful and attentive. In a few moments, it was over. Leonard Crow Dog stood before David.

"Gray Wolf Clear Water will have his ship," Leonard Crow Dog said. "He will find it."

When I heard this story much later, I thought of two things. One was that, if we had not stopped to cavort with the turtles, we would have been about four hours ahead of where we actually were, and we would have missed out on what was to be the greatest experience of my life. The other was that the turtle is a sacred symbol in the mythology of almost all North American Indians.

On Sunday, July 15, 1979, at about one o'clock in the afternoon, I made spaghetti in the galley and went to the wing of the bridge to eat lunch. It was a blowy, blustery day, and one of my less-seasoned crew members was hanging over the side.

"Ship . . . ship over there," he mumbled, as if with his dying breath.

I dug into my spaghetti. To the man on watch, Alex Hamilton, I yelled, "See that ship?" He yelled back that he certainly did. A few minutes passed while I finished off my lunch. And then I figured it was time to investigate the ship.

"Let's go take a look," I shouted to Alex. And then I went topside to see for myself. I looked and I shouted again. "It's a whaler!"

The ship was about four miles off, and it was unmistakably a whaler. I could make out the catwalk running from her bridge past the mast with its crow's nest to the bow, where the harpooner was visible behind his gun. She was a whaler and she was working.

"A Spanish whaler," I thought. "Maybe we can do something to her. God knows what, but something."

As we got closer, I could see she had stopped whaling and was following a course that would take her to Leixoes, Portugal. We charged after her, at an angle that would help us intercept, for we were clearly able to outrun her. We were doing seventeen knots. She was doing much less. I had guessed right: We were faster than the whalers.

Yet, it took a long time—four hours—for us to overtake her. As we caught up and passed her, cutting across her bow, I cried out:

"My God! It's the *Sierra!*"

13

The Confrontation

"RAM HER! RAM THE *Sierra,* PAUL!"

As we rushed ahead in a choppy, chilly sea at nearly fifteen knots, some of my crew members shouted at me to crash headlong into the pirate whaler, then and there.

They had forgotten that I had sworn not to endanger any lives. Our plan was to confront the *Sierra* outside the harbor at Oporto, and to ram her in such a way that no crew members would be hurt. How could I justify causing the deaths of seamen, either those on board the *Sierra* or among my own crew?

We pulled in behind the *Sierra,* moving along smoothly in the wake that flattened a path for us in the roughly pitching ocean. And then we pulled around her, showing our superiority in size, weight, and speed.

We were in front of the *Sierra* now, directly in front of her.

"Slow down," I ordered.

David Sellers, our captain, gave the signal to the engine room. We cut our speed until we wallowed almost dead in the water, and the *Sierra* bore down on us, on a collision course.

The *Sierra* came at us, looming larger at an alarming rate. She seemed intent on plowing right over us. I could see her bridge clearly, and the men there, a half dozen or so, were staring at us, some with binoculars, and I could sense their tension. The *Sierra* kept coming, and then, almost too late, she veered to starboard. She missed us by a few yards.

We fell behind her again and continued the harassment. She pushed on at high speed, breaking the waves over her bow and across the catwalk to the bridge. We cruised serenly in her wake. Occasionally, just to annoy, we would speed up and make a run at her. We took photographs of the crewmen who came to the stern to stare at us.

We tailed the *Sierra* all night long, until we both came within sight of the lights of Leixoes, Portugal. At about three o'clock in the morning, the *Sierra* killed her engines and simply drifted. We did the same, keeping an eye out for untoward movements. When the *Sierra* started up and shifted position, we did the same.

At about ten in the morning, the pilot from Leixoes came aboard, and I told him, "I don't want to go in yet, not until the *Sierra* goes in." He said a pilot also was aboard the *Sierra* and was preparing to take her into the harbor. He added, "I can't stay on here all day. If you don't go in now, you probably won't be able to get in today. Why don't you both go in together?" That made sense. The pilot had an honest face, and David Sellers and I felt there was no reason for him to mislead us. We agreed, and he took us in the half-mile.

We tied up at Pier One. The immigration officer came aboard with the agent assigned to us at our radioed request. The immigration officer and the pilot engaged in a spirited conversation in Portuguese, laughing so much that my curiosity was aroused. I asked the agent what was going on.

"The pilot laughs because the *Sierra* is not coming

in," the agent said. "He tells the immigration officer he
fooled you. He says *Sierra* leaves at two o'clock this afternoon."

"Where are they going?"

"Destination unknown."

I demanded immediate clearance. The immigration
man said I would have to wait until four o'clock. That
would give the *Sierra* a two-hour headstart, which would
be intolerable. I might be able to figure out where she
was headed—an African port, perhaps, or some place
in Spain—but if those guesses proved wrong, I might
spend weeks or months trying to catch up with her
again.

"Look, nobody on this ship has set foot ashore," I
argued. "There is no reason why you can't clear us right
now and let us be on our way, too."

"Not until four o'clock."

"Why four o'clock?"

No answer. I was flooded with suspicion. Were the
Portuguese conspiring to stall us long enough for the
Sierra to escape? It seemed unlikely. But there was no
way I could test whether or not I had simply become
ensnarled in innocent but deadly bureaucratic red tape.
It was the lunch hour, and nothing would happen in
Leixoes until at least two o'clock. By that time, the *Sierra*
would be gone.

"Oh, my God," I thought. "Have I chased this killer
all this way just to have a Portuguese official fake me
out? This is ridiculous."

I called Captain Sellers aside as soon as the pilot, the
immigrations man, and the agent had gone ashore.

"I'm going to do the job now," I said.

"But what about clearance?" David objected. "How
can you leave without clearance?"

"I'm going to make a run for it during lunch hour,"

I said. "You could hold up every bank in town and stroll away during lunch hour. Nobody's going to be alive again until two o'clock."

I told David that I would not ask, or even permit, him to risk the loss of his master's license by breaking maritime law. He started arguing that he was the only truly experienced seaman aboard besides me and the only one with a master's license, and that, without him, the whole operation would be in serious jeopardy. I cut him off. I said there was no time to argue. He was simply to pack up and get off the ship, making sure he reported immediately to Portuguese authorities that he had lost his command before the *Sea Shepherd* made her unauthorized departure. Reluctantly, he agreed, and he went below to pack.

Jacques Longini and Paul Condon had left the ship in the Azores. With Captain Sellers leaving, seventeen of us remained. We assembled on deck, and I spelled out the situation: we had found the *Sierra* despite all the odds against us; we had held off ramming her at sea for fear of costing lives; we had intended ramming her against the stone and concrete wharves of Leixoes; but now—with the *Sierra* about to slip away—the situation was more desperate, and we would have to take more desperate measures. There was now far less risk because we were so close to shore, but I emphasized that the price still might be higher than some might care to pay: death or imprisonment.

I offered my crew members a choice: to remain on board or to leave. Fourteen decided that what had seemed so noble and adventurous back in Boston, where it was all highly theoretical, had a different aspect at high noon here in Leixoes. I gave them ten minutes to pack, and, in less time than that, they had disembarked and were standing on the pier among their belongings. They looked quite bewildered. Captain Sellers took charge immediately, using money I had given him to pay for everybody's transportation home.

I was disappointed by some of the resignations, surprised by others, and relieved by still others. But the two who remained and stood by me proved to be an inspiration—so cool were they under pressure and so capable that they seemed to be doing the work of many, even at the most crucial times. These two—Chief Engineer Peter Woof and Third Engineer Jerry Doran—had been my most dependable crew members all along, cheerful and uncomplaining, totally dedicated. Now they were with me to attempt to do the impossible. I was determined to man our ship with only three hands.

Without Peter and Jerry, I could not have gone on. Outwardly, I tried to appear as sure of myself as they seemed to be, even though my mouth was so dry that I could hardly speak, and I was assailed by a barrage of fears—fear of failing, fear of dying, and, not least of all, fear of spending the rest of my life in a Portuguese prison.

It was half past noon on Monday, July 16, 1979. We cast off, and, while Captain Sellers yelled instructions at us from the dock, we three hopped about like cats on a hot tin roof, trying to do the work of a full crew, maneuvering painfully in the cramped quarters around Pier One, and slowly, slowly heading out of the harbor without a pilot, without clearance, and without any assurance that we could sail in any fashion with so few hands.

As we approached the harbor entrance, we picked up speed. By the time we reached the mouth, we were moving at a headlong dash, charging toward our rendezvous with the *Sierra*. We could see her as we broke free of the harbor. She was about a quarter of a mile away, drifting. Her crew, for the most part, was lounging on deck. I could barely make out the faces. One man saw us and pointed. Others joined him, smiling and jabbering excitedly.

Peter was in the engine room. Jerry was on the bridge with me. I was steering with one hand and trying to take pictures with the other. We were set on full speed ahead, but we were still gathering speed, and I doubt that we ever went faster than twelve knots.

"Here, Jerry," I said, as the *Sierra* loomed dead ahead. "You take the pictures and I'll steer."

"I don't know how to take pictures," he said.

"Okay, then, I'll take the pictures and you steer."

"I don't know how to steer," he said.

Peter was reluctant to exceed twelve knots, and I often wonder what would have happened if we had been going all out—say, seventeen knots. We might have sheared the *Sierra's* bow clean off.

The ship was much nearer now, and I could see the crewmen's faces clearly. I could even make out Captain Arvid Nordengen, the big Norwegian skipper, looking at us with fierce intensity. A man standing next to him was holding what looked like a rifle.

We made straight for the *Sierra.* My intention was to try to crash our bow into her bow in such a way that the harpoon gun would be cut away. I did not want to hit too hard. I knew from past experience at sea and in trying to break through the ice of the Gulf of St. Lawrence that collisions at sea could send people flying about like rocks in a tin can. I did not want to hurt anyone—not so much because I had tender feelings toward the forty-two men aboard the *Sierra,* but because I oppose causing injury to any living thing and because their injuries might provide an excuse for a backlash that could undermine whatever good will our dramatic and dangerous aggression might produce.

It was difficult to aim our bow with precision. We were 779 tons, and it is a long way from the bridge, where I stood, to the bow. I could not see the point of the bow, and I had to estimate where it was. As it turned out, I was off by about six inches.

We hit. We hit just behind the harpoon gun's platform at the bow, and we kept on going. I was surprised at how lightly we felt the impact in the wheelhouse. But there was plenty of damage where the two ships had come together.

About four feet of the gunwale plate was torn and bent outwardly at the bow, and aft of that for about twenty feet the upper part of the hull was buckled inwardly where we had struck at an angle and run up to the bow.

As we bounced apart, I threw the rudder hard to starboard, beginning a tight 360-degree turn that would line us up on the *Sierra* for a second ramming. This time, we would go for broke. The first collision was a warning, to arouse the crew. And we had plenty of evidence that it served its purpose. Men were popping out of hatches and running up and down ladders like termites in a turned-over log. Nobody on the *Sierra* was laughing now. The man with the rifle had raised it and had aimed it our way just as we hit. I could not see him at all as we arced for the second hit, making a complete circle around the pirate ship.

The men aboard the *Sierra* were bracing themselves for the second collision. The first one had caught them completely by surprise, and they were not to make that mistake again. But there was little they could do. My guess was that, in the minute or so it took us to go around the *Sierra*'s stern, her crew in the engine room worked frantically to get up her engines. But she was still dead in the water as we lined up on her.

Just before we hit, I looked around and saw Peter Woof standing on the bridge next to Jerry. I had just yelled down to him, "Give me more revs!" And here he was, standing directly behind me.

"What are you doing here?" I asked.

He tore his eyes from the *Sierra* long enough to shoot me an indignant and incredulous glare.

"Do you think I'm crazy? Do you think I'm going to stay down there in the engine room when we hit and that engine goes flying off its mount? Forget it!"

We had had no experience in ramming. We all expected that, as in an automobile crash, we would go flying about when the collision came. Jerry and I had brought mattresses up to the bridge, for protection when we hit the *Sierra*. I had forgotten about it the first time, when we struck a glancing blow as a warning. Now I remembered it as we drew within a few feet of our quarry the second time. I realized that, while Jerry was holding his mattress, Peter had mine, and I had none.

We hit the *Sierra* amidships this time, but again at an angle, purposely, because we did not want to get stuck. We felt her 683 tons sag under the weight of our larger vessel, and she keeled over to her starboard. Our bow plates were three-quarters of an inch thick. They tore open from the impact, but our bow chopped into the *Sierra*'s side like a hatchet. It ripped her open—a huge gash six feet wide and eight feet long—and we could see the contraband whalemeat in her guts. Again we were on top of her, dug into her at a sharp angle, and, with our engines pushing us into a tighter angle, our starboard side scissored into her port side with a loud bang. We stove in about forty-five feet of her hull but left our hull unmarked.

Still churning ahead, the *Sea Shepherd* tossed the *Sierra* aside and pulled away. My crew of two and I were full of fight now. Damaging the whaler would not be enough. We wanted her on the bottom.

We went around for a third ramming. We had jabbed, we had hooked, and now would come the knockout blow. If possible, I would cut her in half this time.

But that was not to be. From a dead stop, the *Sierra*'s engineers cranked her up to full speed, and she raced for the mouth of the harbor. By the time we had come about, she was well on her way. Taking on water and listing heavily to port, the *Sierra* scuttled past the breakwaters and into the mouth of the harbor at Leixoes. We chased for a while, but then we broke off, realizing that we could not catch her before she mingled with the innocent ships inside.

Peter immediately set a course for England—the *Sea Shepherd*'s run for freedom. We realized that our chances of escaping were not very good. We sailed north along the coast of Portugal for four hours. So far, there was no pursuit, and we began to think that we might actually luck out. But then, eight miles short of Spanish territorial waters, a Portuguese destroyer suddenly appeared off our stern. Our hearts sank as a voice called out for us to stop.

Peter, Jerry, and I conferred. Should we comply? Or should we make a dash for it? Peter was for stalling until we could somehow work our way into Spanish waters, where the Portuguese would have no authority. I had little hope of success, but tried to bluff it anyway.

"This is the *Sea Shepherd*," I said, with as much authority as I could muster. "We are on our way to Britain. I suggest you let us proceed. I would not like to involve Portugal in this affair. We will turn ourselves over to British authorities."

There was a brief silence. Then the Portuguese captain made his reply in softly accented English.

"You want I should fire my guns?"

"No," I said. "That won't be necessary. Hold on one minute and we'll give you an answer."

The three of us talked again. It would take us three days to sail to England, three of us who had not slept in thirty hours doing the work of a full crew. We would have to thread our way through increasingly heavy shipping traffic, and we would not be able to get much sleep to carry us through such an ordeal. Further, we felt our cause was righteous and our actions justifiable. Rather than martyring ourselves to the guns of the Portuguese Navy, perhaps it would be more worthwhile, we thought, to use the incident as a publicity forum from which to challenge the whaling industry even more forcefully.

We told the Portuguese destroyer we would return to Leixoes, and so we did. The warship followed us like a police patrol car all the way.

Jerry began to worry about Portuguese imprisonment. He told us he was afraid of the possibility of torture and brutality. He came up with an idea for escape.

"I'll throw some garbage over the side, and then I'll jump in with a cardboard box over my head," he said. "I'll float right by them, wait until I'm alone, and swim for shore. It's twenty miles, but I can make it."

"You'll float right into that destroyer's props," Peter hooted. "She'll spit you out in little pieces."

We arrived back in harbor about nine o'clock that night. We sailed as slowly as we could past the *Sierra*, which was a wreck, twisted and showing a thirty-degree list. Her crew, on the deck and roof of the bridge, yelled and screamed and cursed at us. We waved back cheerfully and made grand bows, as one does to acknowledge bravos for a fine performance, and we threw them an obscene hand gesture or two for good measure.

We were ordered to tie up at the opposite end of the harbor from the *Sierra*. Surprisingly, we were not placed under arrest. We were free to come and go as we liked, at least for the time being. The port police captain suggested I might be charged with negligence, but I insisted I was not negligent at all, having rammed the *Sierra* on purpose.

The Portuguese, while deciding what to do with us, made sure that we did not make any more unauthorized departures. They put the *Sea Shepherd* on the other side of a low drawbridge, so that, without permission, we could have escaped only by scraping off our superstructure. And the authorities confiscated our passports. British Consul Ian Murray dropped by once to discuss our status, and, with obvious reference to escape, he said, "Don't do what I think you're thinking of doing."

But the Portuguese were not interested in me or Peter or Jerry. The principle in maritime law they were following has to do with treating a vessel as if it were a human being. It is the ship that commits the offense, not the people aboard. Thus, the authorities at Leixoes were holding the *Sea Shepherd* for the offense of ramming the *Sierra*, and what we had to do now was figure out some way of setting her free.

Starlet had told me, when I called her by telephone, that we were getting heavy publicity, not only in Vancouver, but throughout the world. She said she had been besieged by the American television networks to arrange for me to appear on camera to explain the whole adventure. Could I come home and do some of this television publicity? While the Portuguese were in the throes of their legal processes over the fate of the *Sea Shepherd,* that seemed like the best possible use of my time. My passport was returned, and I hired a ship's agent to look after our interests, and flew to New York for television appearances and then returned to Vancouver. I assured the Portuguese authorities that I would be back for the *Sea Shepherd.* I hired guards and posted them at the dock to keep watch over her.

Meanwhile, Jerry and Peter had lost patience with the legal and bureaucratic maneuvering. With their passports still not returned, both came to me and announced they were going to take their chances on an unauthorized departure.

Jerry hitchhiked a ride to the Rio Miño, which forms part of Portugal's border with Spain, and swam across it. Later, he joked that he was probably the first American wetback ever to enter Spain.

Peter bought a bicycle and went pedaling away. Two weeks later, David Sellers opened the front door of his home forty miles north of Inverness in Scotland, and there was Peter, his bicycle parked nearby. He flashed a grin and said,

"Got a cup of tea, Skipper?"

14

The Way Ahead

IT WAS EARLY IN THE MORNING OF Tuesday, July 17, 1979, and Cleveland Amory, founder and president of the Fund for Animals, was sound asleep in his New York City apartment. The rude jangling of the bedside telephone woke him with a start. It was the Associated Press. The *Sea Shepherd,* which his organization had bought for $120,000, had rammed the whaler *Sierra* several hours earlier and was under arrest in Portugal. Would he have any comment?

Even half asleep, Amory retained his journalist's instincts. First, some facts. Exactly what had happened? The AP reporter told him the ramming had occurred a quarter-mile from shore and nobody was killed or hurt. Relief flooded his 260-odd-pound frame, and, in that radio announcer's voice of his, he did indeed have a statement:

"We cannot condone ramming ships in the open ocean. But this apparently was done so skillfully and conscientiously that we cannot have anything but admiration at the care that was taken to avoid harming any living thing. As to legality, the pirate whaling ship *Sierra* has been operating illegally for the past ten years."

Later, I was to learn that Cleveland was not surprised that we had rammed the *Sierra,* and he was "thrilled at the disciplined heroism" (his exact words) the three of us showed in operating a large boat that normally required at least eight people to start, and, secondly, in doing so without death or injury. We talked by telephone shortly after the ramming. He said he was proud that we had exercised prudence in following his basic rules: Don't drown, don't get off the boat, don't hurt anybody, and don't get arrested. The getting-arrested part was still up in the air—and I had never been too good at avoiding arrest, anyway—but I figured three out of four was not bad, and I gratefully accepted the praise on behalf of Peter, Jerry, and myself.

I hired a West German national named Axel Wolter as our ship's agent in Leixoes to look after the *Sea Shepherd* and to see to guards and lawyers and the whole rigmarole of Portuguese bureaucracy—maritime and legal. Then I flew back to North America to tackle the news media. To my surprise, I was something of a celebrity. The ramming had stirred interest among reporters in both the print and electronic media, and I did my best to tell our story at every opportunity.

Back in Vancouver, Starlet and I had a happy reunion. To tell the truth, I really had no certainty that I would survive the confrontation with the *Sierra*. Doing so, and returning to Starlet, who had been so uncomplainingly supportive during the entire ordeal, brought me more happiness than I had had any reason to expect. As it usually is with one consumed by his work, it never occurred to me to be concerned about a personal life. With Starlet, who seemed as engrossed in my projects as I was, the problem never arose. Whatever we did, we did together.

The news from Portugal was up and down throughout the summer and fall of 1979. Our agent would send word that the authorities were about to make a pronouncement on the fate of the *Sea Shepherd;* I would fly over to be on hand for that, only to be told after arrival that there had been a delay of some kind. This happened about three times, until, finally, we got the bottom line: We could have the boat back upon payment of $750,000 in damages and fine to the port authorities, or she would be turned over to the Sierra's owners, who could do with her as they wished. Presumably, we would still owe the fine.

It was quite a dilemma. How could we raise $750,000? And why should we pay that much for a boat that had cost us $120,000? And, if we let her go, our beautiful *Sea Shepherd* might be changed into an ugly whaling boat, killing instead of protecting the whales.

On December 29, 1979, in response to cables from me, David Greenway and David McColl flew to Oporto from England, and Peter Woof and his girl friend, Lins Masterton, came all the way from Australia. We met on the dock at Leixoes. We took stock. The guards I had hired were nowhere to be seen, and even a quick look around told us that the *Sea Shepherd* was being systematically looted. Peter, my mechanical wizard, undertook an inventory to determine (a) precisely what had been taken away, and (b) what we needed to get the engines started in the event—just in case—we decided to try to make a run for it again.

We had missed it on our first day aboard, but on the second day, December 30, we spotted our two-ton air compressor lashed to the deck of the *Zacoroula,* a Cyprus-registered cargo ship docked next to us. We had to go across her to get ashore, which was how we made the discovery. Checking around, we found other equipment of ours, including our ship's bell. Infuriated, we began collecting what we could, and wondered how to get the bigger stuff back aboard the *Sea Shepherd.*

Suddenly, we were accosted by a watchman, who shouted and rushed at us. Three other men materialized, and we were in a genuine Donnybrook. We were flailing away at one another when one man broke away, ran into a cabin and came out with a flare gun—our own flare gun stolen from the *Sea Shepherd*—which he aimed at us. I had a slingshot with me, and I let fly with a stone that caught the fellow in the chest. That seemed to end the fight.

We made our way to the office of the port police for help. My heart sank when I saw our single-sideband radio in the dockside office. With the police among the looters, what chance would I have of getting our gear back, or even of proving it was ours? We went through the motions of reporting what we knew anyway, and we were told, "You're in enough trouble already—don't make more!" We borrowed the telephone and made a call to British Consul Ian Murray, who promised to come around and see us the next day.

Back aboard the *Sea Shepherd,* we continued our inventory. Peter and I used blow torches to cut away doors and hatches that had been welded shut by the port authorities. We worked furiously on the auxiliary engines until, finally, Peter got one going enough so that we could run the generator that gave us enough light to see by in the engine room. But we could only do that for ten or twenty minutes because a water pump, rusted shut, would not work enough to keep the engine from overheating. Yet, we were able to assess generally what we were missing: about a hundred tons of Diesel fuel, dozens of critical sections of three-inch copper fuel lines, the main compressor, and a discouragingly large number of pumps and valves. Peter estimated that it would take two to three weeks to get the boat seaworthy.

All during December 31, 1979, as the Portuguese ashore cranked up for what proved to be a noisy and bibulous welcome to the New Year, Peter, Lins Masterton, and I worked in the engine room. We would get an auxiliary engine started enough to generate electricity and light, only to have it fail because of some rusted-up part. We nibbled on cookies and sipped tea from a café ashore, but our strength and determination were ebbing. On the plus side, I discovered that our navigation equipment was in the office of our agent, Axel Wolter, who said he was holding it for safekeeping. We were pleased, too, to have a visit, as promised, from British Consul Murray. But that went awry when he recognized Peter, whose passport he still held from the last visit.

"Hel-lo, there, Peter!" Murray said with heavy cordiality. "You back again? Got new documents, have we? Have you informed the Portuguese authorities you are here?"

In his almost incomprehensible back-country Australian Peter mumbled something about having filled in the usual immigration and customs forms. But he shot me a look that said we had to act fast now. Murray advised us to get out of Portugal again, and quickly.

Murray had a harbor policeman with him and the two of them escorted David McColl and David Greenway to the dock. They had to cross the deck of the *Zacoroula,* whose crewman sat around glowering at all of us. Peter, Lins, and I, alone on the *Sea Shepherd* now, held a council of war. We knew it was a time for decision. Our options were few.

"Peter, I don't want these bastards to take the whole ship," I said. "I don't want them to turn her into a goddam whaler, either."

"I agree," Peter said.

"Do you think we could light a fire and cause hopeless damage before those Cypriots or somebody else can come back and take her over?"

"Well, I have an aversion to fire," Peter said.

"Scuttle?"

"Scuttle."

I got a screwdriver and took the ship's plaque, the brass nameplate, down from the captain's quarters. I put it in my duffle bag. I took down the British ensign, the ship's flag, and folded it gently and put that in the bag, too, to be used one day on another *Sea Shepherd,* I knew.

It was about 9:30 P.M. when Peter stripped off all his clothes, to keep them dry because they were the only clothes he had, and felt his way blindly in the dark down the ladder into the engine room. Peter had spent so much time there—he loved it, really, as a master chef might love his kitchen—that he could simply feel his way. The engine room was pitch black, but he made his way easily to the starboard weed box—a pot-shaped device that contains a strainer through which sea water passes but which keeps out weeds, fish, and debris; the sea water continues through pipes that cool the engines and their lubricating oil.

With a screwdriver, Peter opened the weed box cover by loosening its two bolts only about four full turns. He was kneeling on the cover. He saw it open about an inch and the water came roaring in. Peter's 132 pounds could not hold the cover down, with the seawater pressing against it at about 190 pounds of pressure.

He was surprised, but then he did his engineer's calculations—a ton a minute; the water would be coming in at that rate—250 gallons of it every minute. While this did not seem like much, he thought it should do the trick.

Peter dried off, dressed, and joined Lins and me for a quick but uneventful departure. As we came abreast of the *Edna* on the dock, a couple of crewmen aboard that American vessel eyed us suspiciously. We had been friendly with them, and they had teased us about what we were going to do. David McColl and David Greenway were with them.

"We're leaving," I said to them.

"What about the boat?" David McColl asked.

"The boat will take care of itself," I said.

"I understand," David McColl said.

Silently, he began loosening the lines of fishing boats that had tied up to the *Sea Shepherd*, and we walked on. Without a word being said, he understood that we did not want those six or seven skiffs to go down, too.

Peter and Lins said goodbye in the street outside the docks, caught a taxi, and took off for the train depot. They urged me to do the same, but I wanted to stay around for the final act. Revelers bumped past us as we parted, Peter and Lins to catch the ten-past-midnight train to Lisbon and then on to Madrid, and I to a hotel, where I flopped for needed sleep. Among my other problems, I had a bad cold.

I rose about 10:30 on New Year's Day 1980. Without stopping for breakfast, I checked out of the hotel and headed for the docks. I did not get out of the taxicab. I did not have to leave it to see what I had come to see.

Black-uniformed soldiers by the dozens, some carrying automatic rifles and all of them looking surly at having to work so early after the festivities of the night before, milled about the dock. They talked in loud voices and they looked excited. I did not want to become involved with them in any way.

Down the dock, past the *Edna* and the *Zacoroula,* I could see my beloved vessel, the *Sea Shepherd.* Never had there been a nobler craft, I felt, for she had done everything I had asked of her and more. Now, I thought I might cry as I looked at her bow pointed almost straight up in the air. She was still sinking. Her stern was resting on the bottom of the harbor, and her bow, aimed skyward like an accusing finger, had not yet settled down. Later, the Portuguese would try to salvage her, and she would capsize completely.

There would be all hell to pay, I knew. I told the taxi driver to take me to Oporto, about twenty miles away, a good fare that made him smile. He drove well and quickly, and I jumped out at the train station, a whole hour early for the train to Lisbon.

I was the first passenger. For a small cash contribution, a station attendant put me on board. I found a dark corner and curled up in it. I watched through a window. I could see much of the passenger section of the depot, but I could not be seen. Within twenty minutes, a truckload of black-uniformed soldiers arrived. They scurried about, setting up checkpoints. They examined the identifications of every passenger boarding the Lisbon train, peered at the papers and then looked hard at the faces of the people. I watched from my hiding place, too tense to smile.

It was late afternoon when we arrived in Lisbon. I had wondered all the way about what I would do when I got there. I knew there was a 7:30 P.M. British Caledonia flight to London and at least two other flights after that—one to South Africa and the other to Brazil. I would board anything I could get. By this time, I realized that Portuguese soldiers in black with automatic rifles would be all over the airport.

It was 8 P.M. when I checked in at the British Caledonia counter, American Express card in hand. The attendant said the plane to London was still on the runway, having been delayed by fuel problems. I could still make it aboard. I bought a ticket.

The blanket of military security had been withdrawn from the British Caledonia facilities when flight time passed for the flight to London. The assumption had been a logical one: the time has come and gone; *ergo,* so has the plane. But it was still on the runway, and I was being whisked to the plane by a very efficient attendant. As we dashed past the airport café, I looked inside and saw six or eight soldiers sipping beer and waiting to check out the next flight at boarding time.

At the immigration desk, I tensed. But the airline attendant was all routine, all brisk efficiency. The immigration officer on duty, unattended by any police or military guard, seemed only mildly interested. He was apparently used to such last-minute sprints. The attendant explained hurriedly in Portuguese that I was running late for the London flight. Casually, almost sleepily, the immigration man opened my passport without looking at the page with my name and picture on it, found a clean page, and stamped it for exit. He waved us on.

The attendant took me all the way out to the Tarmac of the airport runway and never left me until I was safely aboard the plane. For the next twenty minutes or so, I sat like a figure carved from stone, waiting guiltily for the hand of Portuguese authority to clap me on the shoulder. At long last, we took off, and, in a very little while, we were at London's Heathrow Airport, and I was free.

Between the time we rammed the *Sierra* and the time we sent the *Sea Shepherd* to the bottom, I had spent most of my time traveling, either back and forth to Portugal or around the United States doing television and newspaper interviews. But we—Starlet and I—had also found time to get married. This we did on October 31, 1979, in Vancouver, with Starlet's sister Jadene as her matron of honor, and Bob Hunter, who had been with me on so many other ventures, as my best man. We also had a pretty good showing of her family and mine, plus friends, also on hand. We have been blessed since then with a baby girl, whom we named Lilliolani. My life is very full now, with my own family and ever-growing responsibilities in the conservation field.

During that period between the ramming and the scuttling I happened to be in Washington, D.C., doing interviews and conferring with Lewis Regenstein, head of the Fund for Animals office there. It was September 3, 1979. I was approached by a European conservationist I have known for a while. He asked me for details on the construction of the *Sierra*—how big was the pirate whaler I had rammed, how thick its plates, where was it docked now? I answered as best I could. The *Sierra* was just under seven hundred tons, her plates at the water line were about three-quarters of an inch thick, and she was being moved to Lisbon for repairs.

The Canadian authorities, meanwhile, had been postponing my trial on charges of interfering with the 1979 seal hunt, and it was clear that the plan was to have me in court when the 1980 hunt got underway. I considered myself fortunate for not having been charged in previous violations of the Seal Protection Act. Now, it seemed that the game plan was to see the whole thing through—and I was finally called to court in Quebec, at the Provincial Court at Perce in the Gaspe District, on February 6, 1980. The magistrate was Judge Yvon Mercier, and the seven other defendants besides myself were my cohorts on the ice: Joe Goodwin, Matt Herron, Keith Krueger, David MacKenney, Paul Pezwick, Eddy Smith, and Mark Sterk.

On the first day of the trial, I was sitting outside the courtroom with a couple of dozen Royal Canadian Mounted Police nearby. The pay telephone a few feet away began to ring. I picked up the receiver. Oddly enough, the call was for me. It was a representative of the Canadian Department of External Affairs, checking up on my whereabouts. The *Sierra,* he said, had been blown sky high in Lisbon harbor and had sunk to the bottom in ten minutes.

"Don't blame me," I said. "I'm sitting here among twenty-five Mounties."

"Well, where's Peter Woof?"

"He's here, too!"

Peter, ever faithful, had flown in from Australia again to be with me and Starlet at the trial.

I was called back into the courtroom, to see what my fate would be for violating the Seal Protection Act the previous spring, wondering furiously how the *Sierra* had met her fate. It would be a while before I learned the whole story.

Meanwhile, I had to concentrate on my trial. It was held entirely in French and the defendants had a hard time following what was going on. On March 11, 1980, I was found guilty of everything I was charged with,

fined, and sentenced to jail. Judge Mercier fined me
$4,000 for violating the Seal Protection Act, $4,000 for
interfering with the seal hunt by throwing dye on the
pups, and $300 for resisting arrest—for a total of
$8,300. The judge said that I had threatened national
security; public interest therefore demanded that the
court make an example of me.

As a result, I was also sentenced to serve ten days in
Orsainville Prison, about eight miles from Quebec
City—the sentence to begin the first day of the 1980 seal
hunt.

My seven colleagues were fined a total of $28,000.

Our lawyer, Jacques Laurin, and Lew Regenstein,
who flew up from Washington, D.C., to give support to
Starlet and me and to pay the fines, were aghast at the
stiff penalties assessed against me. And there was more.
Judge Mercier also ordered me to stay away from the
seal hunt for three years. If I refused to sign an agreement to do that, he said, I would have to serve another
three months in jail. This probation order was entirely
in French, as were all the records of proceedings. I was
not given a translation in English. When I asked for
one, the judge said that, in Quebec, one spoke French,
and, if I did not sign the agreement, I would get an
additional fifteen days in jail for contempt. At the urging of Cleveland Amory, I signed the paper. But I do
not consider that I agreed to anything, for I signed a
paper that I could not read.

At the prison, I did not serve the full ten days that
had been levied. I served for seven days, and I was told
that I had three days off for good behavior. The jailer
came to me and said, "Pack up your bags and get lost."

It was a mixed blessing. There was a blizzard going
outside, and it was eight miles to the city. I had a suitcase

to carry, with no transportation lined up, and only a light sports coat to keep me warm. Also, I was weak after being on a hunger strike at the prison for five days. Luckily, I had walked only about a mile in the storm before a motorist came by and picked me up.

It was not until the summer of 1980, while I was attending the International Whaling Conference at Brighton, England, as an observer, that I picked up details of how the *Sierra* was blown up. It seems this is what happened:

Two men and a woman went to Lisbon. While the woman stood guard, the two men "borrowed" a skiff in the harbor and rowed silently across the water to the *Sierra,* tied up in the Tagus River. All three wore wet-suits, almost invisible on that dark night of February 5, 1980.

At the *Sierra,* on the side of the hull nearest the dock, the two men located the area of the refrigerator room, the large open space inside the ship where the whale-meat is stored during operations. They dove some six feet below the water line and quickly attached a mag-netic mine. As best they could, in the underwater dark-ness, they set the timing device for 6:15 A.M. the next day.

The two men swam to the surface, got back into their skiff and rowed, as silently as they had come, to another part of the docks, where the woman waited. They stripped off their wetsuits, keeping out of sight under the wharves, and changed into traveling clothes. The trio then caught a taxicab to the Lisbon railroad depot, where they boarded the midnight train to Spain.

At 6:17 A.M., as Lisbon still slept, the *Sierra* ex-ploded. A ten-foot hole was blown in her hull. In ten minutes, she turned upside down and sank.

At 10 A.M., from a village on the Spanish side of Spain's border with Portugal came a telephone call to the office of the United Press International in Lisbon. The caller, a woman, said,

"The *Sea Shepherd* is avenged! Make no mistake about it—this was no accident, this was a deliberate act of sabotage! The *Sierra* will kill no more whales! We did it for the *Sea Shepherd!*"

That was the *coup de grace* against the outlaw whalers, for the *Sierra*'s owners could collect insurance only in the event of an accident. For sabotage, there was no payoff.

And there was more. Shortly after the ramming of the *Sierra*, the South African government seized and impounded the pirate whalers *Susan I* and *Theresa III*. On April 27, 1980, the *Isba I* and the *Absa II*, two of Spain's five whalers, blew up and sank in the harbor of Marin near Vigo, Spain—victims of magnetic mines, one of them homemade, which had been planted by the same trio that destroyed the *Sierra*. Finally, the pirate whaler *Astrid*, which had changed its name from *Cape Fisher*, idled in the Canary Islands, unable to sign on a crew there after we posted signs offering a twenty-five thousand dollar reward to anybody who could sink her. She has since been sold to a Korean fishing firm to be converted into a trawler, and the reward offer as a consequence was withdrawn.

All of these actions, I am proud to say, took place without loss of life or injury to the crews of the ships involved.

Yet, cetaceans continue to be killed along with other wildlife that are forced by man to die needlessly. Some six million dolphins have died in the last decade and a half after being netted by U.S. tuna fishermen in the eastern Pacific. Although the carnage has been reduced, over ten thousand are still being killed each year.

I have no death wish, as I am often accused of having. I have fought with all my might to stay alive on those occasions that I felt death was near. I would like to live to a productive old age—together with my wife, Starlet, to see my daughter, Lilliolani, grow up, and maybe some other children, too, and grandchildren as well. But I must die some day. And when I do, an epitaph that said I fought to save the whales and the seals and all the creatures of the earth would not be too bad a thing.

That is what I will be doing—fighting for the whales until there are either no more whalers or no more whales. I will be doing that, and I will be continuing to worry about this:

We know what killing the whales is doing to the whales. But what is it doing to us?

Index